AN INSIDER'S GUIDE TO

BETTER
NURSING
HOME
CARE

AN INSIDER'S GUIDE TO

BETTER NURSING HOME CARE

75 TIPS
YOU SHOULD KNOW

DONNA M. REED

Prometheus Books

59 John Glenn Drive
Amherst, New York 14228-2119

Published 2009 by Prometheus Books

Inquiries should be addressed to
Prometheus Books
59 John Glenn Drive
Amherst, New York 14228-2119
VOICE: 716-691-0133, ext. 210
FAX: 716-691-0137
WWW.PROMETHEUSBOOKS.COM

13 12 11 10 09   5 4 3 2 1

Library of Congress Cataloging-in-Publication Data

Reed, Donna M., 1962–
    An insider's guide to better nursing home care : 75 tips you should know / Donna
M. Reed.
        p. cm.
    ISBN 978-1-59102-671-6 (pbk : alk paper)
    1. Nursing home care—Evaluation. 2. Nursing homes—Evaluation. 3. Long-term care
facilities—Evaluation. 4. Patient satisfaction. 5. Patients—civil rights. I. Title.

RA997.R44 2008
362.16068'3—dc22

2008051669

Printed in the United States on acid-free paper

For my mother, Nancy Spaniol, five-time cancer survivor, and my father, Donald Spaniol, Vietnam veteran of three tours. And for all of our parents and grandparents, may their future battles be easily conquered.

CONTENTS

ACKNOWLEDGMENTS

I want to thank my biggest supporter, Jeff Larrabee, who is in large part responsible for the creation of this book. Several years ago, he happened to ask me about my workday at the nursing home. I replied, "Well, I could write a book about my day." He said, "Why don't you?" Since that day, he has devoted many, many hours to proofreading and editing this book. I couldn't have done it without his help. Thank you for always being there.

Thanks to my son, Ricky, who has been helping me every step of the way with issues big and small.

I was very lucky to have a computer genius available any time of the day or night to help me through more than one technological crisis. Thanks to Jim Pratt for helping me through this project and for being the great friend that he's been for the past twenty years.

I am extremely grateful to my former co-workers who took an interest in this book and provided insightful suggestions. Thanks to Cindy Piper, RN, Denise Marden, LPN, Laurie Ke, RN, and Shelley Richardson, RN, who managed to make even the longest, most under-staffed nursing home shifts enjoyable.

Thank you to James (Rusty) Pratt, Sallie Nifong, Lisa Tilley, Finis Williams, Esq., and Cecile Reed, who proofread and offered their valuable opinions.

Thank you to everyone at Prometheus Books for making this book a reality, especially Julia DeGraf and Steven L. Mitchell.

15

INTRODUCTION

I wrote this book because while I was working as a nursing home nurse, I saw firsthand how most residents received substandard care on a regular basis. I became disgusted with the way elderly residents are treated in most nursing homes. I was certain that families needed to know exactly what was happening to their loved ones and what they could do to improve their nursing home care. I wrote this book because I wanted to tell the truth about nursing homes.

I worked in the same nursing home for three years while I attended law school. But before law school and for a period of time afterward, I worked as an agency, or "temp," nurse. Throughout my time as an agency nurse, I was sent to several different nursing homes and I was able to see the similarities in each of the homes I visited. I soon realized that nursing homes are all pretty much the same: understaffed and in violation of many of the rights enacted to protect elderly residents.

I met many caring nurses and nursing assistants during my ten years as a nursing home nurse. There are many, many nursing home employees who have only the residents' best interests at heart. I believe that the vast majority of nursing home employees are devoted to providing the best care possible, but when faced with the impossible task of caring for too many residents with inadequate staffing levels, they fail. For the most part, the employees of the nursing home are not the primary cause of the inadequate care.

As you read this book you should be aware of a few important Nursing Home 101 basic truths. The first thing you need to know, and I cannot stress this enough, is that most nursing homes are severely understaffed. This is the main reason for poor care. They are understaffed because the nursing home industry (in almost every state) is not bound by any legal standard that would mandate a specific staffing requirement, so facilities are free to value profit over adequate nursing care. There is no federal law to tell nursing homes how many nurses and nursing assistants they must have on duty for a certain number of residents, although a few states have enacted their own staffing standards. Because most facilities employ a small number of nursing personnel to care for a large number of residents, many shortcuts must be taken during the delivery of nursing care.

The second thing you need to know is that nursing home nurses are trained and encouraged to conduct nursing business in a manner that protects the facility. Nurses are coached on what to say to family members and what to document in the medical record. I will show you in great detail how to get the information you need in spite of a system that will seem to be working against you.

The third thing you need to understand is that nursing home care is delivered in an assembly line fashion. The staff move quickly and they usually require the residents to pick up the pace as well. For the most part, care is delivered systematically and robotically in the name of speed and convenience—that is, the convenience of the staff.

Finally, I must warn you that if you choose to implement each and every suggestion that I put forth, you will feel as though you have taken on a full-time job. But once the nursing home staff understands that you are an integral, proactive participant on a relentless quest for good nursing home care, they will raise their level of care for your loved one.

Although it may seem like a daunting and perhaps overwhelming prospect to assume the role of advocate for your nursing home resident, I promise you that this book will help you to understand how nursing homes operate, will identify the major reasons why nursing homes have and perhaps deserve their poor reputations, and will show you how to get better care.

I understand that you could be seeking better care for your mother, aunt, grandfather, sister, or uncle; however, to simplify the identification of each possible relative every time I make reference to your loved one, I simply use the word *parent*. I apologize for the generic title, but this prevents you from having to read through a string of nouns each time I make that reference.

Since most nursing home residents live in a long-term-care facility (described in chapter 1), this book focuses on the improvement of care in those nursing homes that provide long-term care. You might also apply many of the suggestions in this book to an assisted-living environment. I will share with you many of my experiences from the nursing homes in which I have worked as I describe the steps you can take to get better care. I will teach you the questions that you need to ask as well as the demands that you need to make in order to ensure safe, high-quality care for your loved one.

I have included a checklist in chapter 8 that outlines the issues you may want to address while assessing your nursing home. The checklist is formatted in a manner that will allow you to keep track of those issues that are acceptable to your loved one and those that need further attention. There are columns for you to place a check mark next to the contact information for the facility to help you tackle each issue.

This book is largely based on my opinion of nursing homes and how I think nursing home care could be improved. The ideas and suggestions herein are based on my own experiences as an employee of or visitor to various nursing homes. I have not been inside every nursing home in the country; therefore, it is impossible for me to comment on the quality of care that is delivered in every nursing home in every state.

CHAPTER 1

NURSING HOME OPERATION

"My greatest fear about aging is that I will someday receive the same quality of nursing home care that is delivered today."
—Donna M. Reed, LPN

All nursing homes are not created equal. Some nursing homes offer luxurious treatment, while most provide only the bare essentials. Some facilities are well staffed, serve great food, and deliver superb care to their residents. Others operate under extremely poor conditions with a low food budget, minimal staff, and inadequate medical supplies. So, how do you find excellence and avoid mediocrity? You fork over at least $100,000 per year and pay an even larger entry fee to live in a private nursing home that does not participate in government-funded programs.

Or, if you are like most Americans, you rely on the assistance of Medicaid and/or Medicare. Most nursing homes are filled with residents who rely on government assistance to pay for at least part of their care. Unfortunately, these are the nursing homes that do not offer luxurious treatment, do not serve great food, and do not deliver superb care to their residents.

The truth is, the delivery of nursing home care is a business. Many of these businesses operate to generate a profit, but even nonprofit nursing homes cut financial corners and divert money from resident care. It may not surprise you to know that many nursing homes and nursing home chains are very successful at reaping hefty annual profits for their owners and investors while paying the managers of these facilities huge salaries. Despite the appearance of overall success, very few nursing homes are successful at consistently delivering commendable care to their residents.

In order to understand how nursing homes operate and deliver care, you must differentiate between the levels of care available in each living situation. Most nursing homes, nonprofit or for-profit, offer at least one of three living situations described in this chapter: assisted living, long-term care, and skilled care. The level of care ranges from minimal assistance for residents who are nearly independent to maximum assistance for residents who cannot feed themselves or go to the bathroom without help.

THREE TYPES OF NURSING HOME LIVING

Assisted Living

Assisted-living facilities provide care to residents who are independent but need some degree of minimal assistance. The care offered is usually very limited. Nursing staff may be on duty part of the day or available on an as-needed basis. Residents who live under this type of arrangement can usually own and operate their own vehicles and leave the grounds unaccompanied whenever they wish.

Many assisted-living residents prepare their own medications. Others may report to a nurse to have them administered. Residents in this living situation may require daily minor medical attention, such as blood pressure or blood sugar checks or assistance with eyedrops. Often, they need no medical care whatsoever but no longer wish to have complete independence.

Long-Term Care

A nursing home that provides full-time partial or total nursing care to residents who are not independent is called a long-term-care facility. Residents who live in this setting have maintenance nursing care available twenty-four hours a day. These residents require help with the basic activities of daily living such as getting dressed, going to the bathroom, eating, and personal hygiene. Medications are delivered to these residents by a nurse or other licensed professional. Confused residents or residents who need to be closely monitored require this level of care.

Some residents who are able to perform most of their own care may live in this setting if they are not quite independent enough for an assisted-living environment. The long-term-care unit is often made up of residents who can express their needs and those who cannot speak at all. Some residents may walk independently or maneuver their own wheelchairs, while others on the same unit may need to be wheeled by staff. Most such settings commonly include a mixture of those who are mentally intact and those who are completely confused. Most nursing homes have their largest number of residents in a long-term-care setting.

Skilled Care

A skilled-care setting, usually called a skilled-care unit or skilled-nursing facility (SNF), is a facility or section of the facility where residents require continuous advanced medical care and receive intensive medical care and rehabilitation. The residents on this nursing unit have either suffered a recent injury, illness, decline in health, and/or are in need of daily rehabilitation. Their days are usually spent with rehabilitation therapists working to improve or restore a prior level of physical capabilities. The goal for residents on the skilled-care unit is to return to their former level of functioning or to determine a new level of ability and learn to function at that level.

The type of care your parent needs, or will need in the future, depends on his or her medical needs, goals, and abilities. Remember that these goals and abilities may change during the time that your parent is in the nursing home, since many people live several years or even decades in a nursing home.

Many nursing homes offer different levels of care within the same building or organization. For instance, your parent could enter the facility as an independent resident (assisted living), but later need more care and transfer to the long-term-care unit without changing nursing homes. Some facilities offer only one or two of the three levels of care, depending on the size and goals of the facility. A facility must be licensed by the state to provide each specific level of care. There are also facilities that are licensed to provide all three levels of care. Because skilled-nursing care requires specialized equipment and staff, it is not offered at every nursing home.

You Should Know whether your facility is licensed to provide skilled care in case your parent ever requires the extra medical care that a skilled-care unit provides. You should know whether your parent will be treated at his or her current nursing home or if he or she will have to be transported to a facility that offers skilled services. Your parent may not currently require such treatment but may in the future. You may be put in the position of temporarily paying for two beds or packing belongings twice if he or she needs to be transferred to another facility.

If your facility has a skilled-care unit, you will want to know if its residents live on the same unit as the long-term-care residents. If your parent, as a long-term-care resident, requires skilled-nursing services at any point during his or her stay, that care may be delivered without having to move your parent to another room. But remember, skilled-unit residents require and receive more care than typical residents on a long-term-care unit. On a long-term-care unit that accepts and mixes skilled-care residents with long-term-care residents, you can be sure that most of the nursing hours allotted for that unit will be directed toward the skilled-care residents and away from the long-term-care residents.

Apart from the three levels of nursing care, many facilities have a nursing unit, which is strictly for residents with Alzheimer's disease. These residents are often in good physical health, but their mental health has deteriorated. Ideally, a nursing home will have a unit specifically devoted to its Alzheimer's residents.

You Should Know whether your facility accepts Alzheimer's or dementia residents regardless of whether or not your parent is afflicted with this disease. Your parent may need to be treated for this disease in the future, and some nursing homes are simply not capable of caring for these types of residents. If your facility admits Alzheimer's residents, your parent may be directly impacted by the facility's living arrangements.

Your parent may live on a unit where both Alzheimer's and non-Alzheimer's residents live, which can be a very difficult arrangement for both types of residents. In these mixed settings, the long-term-care residents are subjected to the behavioral incidents common in Alzheimer's residents, while Alzheimer's residents are subjected to the rigid care routine of the long-term-care unit to which they cannot conform.

Some facilities accept Alzheimer's residents into the general resident population and attempt to treat them in the same manner as the other residents are treated despite the need of Alzheimer's residents for additional, specialized treatment that typical long-term-care residents do not require. Long-term-care units are usually not staffed to meet the unique needs of Alzheimer's residents. Alzheimer's residents tend to wander around and take things that belong to other residents. They urinate in the halls. They remove items off the walls and out of drawers and can sometimes become violent. They need constant supervision, and that means additional staff members.

I have worked on Alzheimer's units where certain residents were known as bullies. These residents wandered around the unit and pushed over anyone in their path. I know of a few residents who suffered broken hips after being pushed to the ground by such residents.

Residents who are known to be violent need constant monitoring. If a facility does not have the staff and resources necessary to prevent injuries to all its residents, the facility may transfer the violent resident to another, more qualified facility. However, it is often not until someone is severely injured that the facility will fully recognize the danger and take appropriate action.

At mealtime on most long-term-care units, the residents who cannot feed themselves are seated around a table and are fed by the staff members. Usually one staff member feeds two or three residents at a time. This arrangement does not always work for Alzheimer's residents who are physically active during mealtime. Many Alzheimer's residents tend to stand during meals, grab food from the plates of other residents, and throw or smear their food. Alzheimer's residents often need to be fed finger food while they are standing or walking since they do not follow traditional meal procedures. The long-term-care unit is not staffed to accommodate the individuality of the typical Alzheimer's resident because each staff member is responsible for feeding and monitoring several residents at once.

Alzheimer's residents function better in an environment that is quiet and less stimulating than most typical long-term units. They need more staff members looking out for their safety and they should be on a locked or alarmed unit to prevent them from wandering away from the facility or to other sections of the nursing home. It can be extremely frustrating or even frightening for a female resident who is completely in charge of her mental faculties to find a male resident standing in her room late at night, especially when she rings her call bell but no one comes to her aid for twenty minutes.

I have also seen Alzheimer's residents unwittingly enter the private living areas of other residents and get yelled at, shooed away, or even beaten after repeatedly being told to leave the room. Alzheimer's residents can be difficult to redirect, and the residents who are lucid often lose their patience trying to defend their own privacy.

It has been my experience that nursing homes with a designated unit or wing specifically for Alzheimer's residents, with adequate staff, are able to deliver better, disease-specific care. Such units provide dementia-friendly surroundings without the noise, chaos, and regimented care associated with the long-term-care unit. When properly managed, the activities and entertainment offered on an Alzheimer's unit usually engage and maintain the residents' attention, which keeps the residents calm and safe.

NURSE-TO-RESIDENT RATIO

The ratio of staff members to residents on each unit will vary from nursing home to nursing home. You will undoubtedly find at most nursing homes that this ratio is consistently far too low. The continued pattern of too few employees caring for too many residents is in desperate need of change. Resident care is not being done safely or efficiently. Everyone complains that there is not enough help, including the residents.

I know of no other profitable business where ignored complaints of inadequate staffing are as frequent among the people who deliver the service as they are among the consumers of the service. The tragedy is that these captive consumers can rarely go elsewhere for their care. The residents are either unable to take their business elsewhere, or all too often, the services are similarly inadequate down the street. With no laws dictating the exact number of employees a nursing home must have on duty at any given time, residents are left complaining while nursing staff hop from job to job in search of better working conditions.

Many nursing home administrators have argued that the reason their facilities are inadequately staffed is because there is a nursing shortage. This is simply not true! The shortage is in the standard of care. Of course nurses will stay away from a facility where so much is expected of them that their nursing licenses are in jeopardy. Any company that treats its employees fairly can hire and retain good employees. I know of too many nursing homes that have raised and met their staffing standards after failing a state inspection to buy into that theory.

You Should Know the nurse-to-resident ratio in your nursing home on every shift, because it indicates how much direct care is delivered to your parent. It stands to reason that if each nurse has to care for thirty residents at facility A, but at facility B the nurses each have a resident load of fifteen, the residents are receiving more nursing attention at facility B. Both the residents and the nurses are probably happier in the environment where the nurses have more time per resident. The most frequent complaint I have heard among nursing home nurses is that there is no time for direct resident care. The direct resident care to which they refer includes treatment of wounds, in-depth evaluation of complaints, helping residents get their exercise, and spending time with residents to determine their overall status.

Nurses also complain specifically that they do not have enough time to do adequate wound treatments. Wound treatments are often done so quickly that a twenty-minute heat or ice treatment is shortened to five minutes, if it is done at all, and a compression bandage that is supposed to be removed and reapplied several times a day is done only once. I know of one nurse who simply writes on the medical record "Treatment not done due to time factor." I have seen many other nurses simply sign their initials that a treatment was done and then actually admit that they did not have the time to do it. The sad truth is, an understaffed facility means more money for the facility.

I have worked in nursing homes with such a low staff-to-resident ratio that the basic needs of the residents were not being sufficiently met. Many residents were not fed their entire meal, properly bathed, or helped to the bathroom in time. On the other hand, I have worked in facilities where the staff-to-resident ratio was appropriate and the workload was therefore quite manageable. The former seems to be the rule while the latter is the exception. In many facilities, everything the nurse does, including passing out the medications, is a race against the clock. She usually completes one task just in time to rush through the next task, usually another medication pass. This, of course, leaves no time for the nurse to converse with residents or assess their individual health concerns. It also leads to errors.

You are probably asking yourself, "What is the appropriate nurse-to-resident ratio?" The answer is, it depends on many factors. It depends on the availability of support staff, the level of care of the residents, the time of day or night, the nursing assistan-to-resident ratio, and the capability of the nursing staff. As you read more, you will learn how to interpret these factors and make a determination for yourself.

Do not be fooled by a nursing home that claims to have an excellent nurse-to-resident ratio, when in fact there may be insufficient support staff, which leaves the nurse wearing many hats in addition to her own. Find out if there is a unit secretary or whether, in the absence of a secretary, the nurse is carrying a telephone in her pocket and has to stop preparing residents' medication to answer it each time it rings (or, more often, whether she must run to the other end of the hall each time it rings). Find out if someone is at the desk doing a portion of the paperwork or if the nurse is responsible for that as well. If there is a unit manager, find out if her office is near the unit she manages or tucked away in an administrative section of the building.

On the evening and weekend shifts, there should be a nursing supervisor on duty. Preferably this nurse is in the building or, at the very least, available by telephone. If there is no supervisor on duty, one of the staff nurses on duty usually assumes the supervisory role. The reason this needs to be factored into your interpretation of the actual staffing ratio is that minor emergencies occur on a constant basis, and it takes valuable time to handle them appropriately.

Incoherent residents often try to leave the building. Staffing shortages fall below the facility standards, and someone needs to stay at the phone for an hour making telephone calls trying to get additional staff to come to work. Plumbing, heating, and electrical emergencies present themselves at all hours of the day or night. These incidents take nursing time and energy away from resident care when the staff nurse is left to pick up the supervisory responsibilities. Is the nurse who is supposed to be taking care of your parent instead on the phone taking care of non-nursing issues?

I once worked at a facility where the roof caved in due to excess snow accumulation. It was an evening shift, and there was no supervisor in the building. Water was pouring into the building, and several rooms needed to be evacuated. The on-call supervisor and the facility administrator were notified by telephone. Not a single additional staff member was sent to the facility and not one management member came to the facility that evening. The incident was handled entirely by the nurses and nursing assistants on duty and, for a brief period of time, the fire department.

The entire wing was in shambles, and many residents had to be moved to new rooms in different sections of the building. There was dust floating in the air, making it impossible to see from one end of the hall to the other. Extension cords were needed for many residents on oxygen concentrators. The medications were late. Residents needed comforting. The telephones were ringing nonstop. I was utterly amazed to learn that we would be completely on our own.

Not all emergencies are of that magnitude and not all will require so much of the nurses' time. But if one of the nurses on duty is expected to handle her nursing assignment of thirty residents *and* the supervisory responsibilities, the facility could be misquoting its staffing ratio, which would be far less than one nurse to thirty residents. Many facilities have made financial cutbacks that include the evening and/or weekend supervisors. Ask the director of your facility who shoulders this responsibility after hours and on weekends.

When determining the actual nurse-to-resident ratio, you also want to be aware of the level of care the residents on your parent's unit require. For example, skilled-care residents often have wounds, fractures, recent strokes, pain, or some other type of new diagnosis that requires frequent assessment, care, and documentation. A skilled-care resident, in my opinion, requires twice as much nursing attention as an average long-term-care resident and should therefore count as two residents when calculating the ratio. To make this calculation, you need to ask the director of nurses (or any nurse on your parent's floor) if skilled-care residents are living with long-term-care residents.

If the answer is no, determining the basic ratio for the long-term-care unit is easy. To determine the average ratio, simply walk the halls of your parent's unit and count the number of beds to learn how many residents are on that unit. The reason that you count the number of beds as opposed to the number of residents is that you want to know the capacity, not the current census. Just because a bed is empty today does not mean that it will remain empty. The facility will not add additional staff members when all of the beds are filled.

Allow yourself at least an hour to count all the nurses. Do it more than once to get a fair average. Also, you will be amazed at how much you can learn by just asking, "How many nurses are on this unit tonight?" You will soon find out which staff members will talk to you about their jobs and which will not. If there are sixty beds on your parent's unit and two nurses, you know that each nurse is caring for thirty residents.

If the answer to whether or not skilled-care residents are living with long-term-care residents is yes, you can obtain only a fluid ratio since skilled-care residents are skilled for only a specified number of allowable days. They may be discharged from the facility after their rehabilitation or, if they remain in the facility, their status may change to a long-term-care resident. This yes or no answer is important because it tells you whether the ratio is somewhat constant or whether it is in constant flux with a primary focus on skilled-care residents. You will need to ask the director or another nurse how many skilled-care residents are on your parent's unit. The division is the same, with the skilled-care residents counting as two residents.

Another factor in determining nurse-to-resident ratio is that not every shift has the same number of staff members since each shift has separate and distinct responsibilities. The day shift gets all of the residents out of bed, dressed, and fed the first two meals. The evening shift focuses on getting everyone to dinner, then undressed and into bed. The overnight shift does not have the responsibility of getting the residents prepared for any regular routine, but this shift can still be busy because the residents must be kept dry throughout the night and not all of the residents sleep through the night. It makes sense that the overnight shift would not need as many staff members as the other two shifts.

You should also take into account that if the nursing assistants are understaffed, the nurse in charge of each shift will have to pick up some of the direct-care duties, leaving her less time to complete her own work. Delivering medication to a resident may turn into assisting the resident in going to the bathroom, helping her get in or out of her clothes, or any number of other duties. If the nurse-to-resident ratio is just barely manageable, helping just a few residents to get dressed could be enough to prevent the nurse from completing her medication pass within the allotted time frame.

Having worked both in nursing homes where the staffing ratio was manageable and where it was not, I have come to my own conclusions as to a reasonable number of residents for one nurse to care for during a shift. If a nurse is doing her own documentation, treatments, and medication passes for her residents, I believe fifteen to twenty-five non-skilled-care residents for a day or evening shift is realistic and safe if the unit is staffed with the appropriate number of nursing assistants.

The only true test to determine the appropriate nurse-to-resident ratio is to know whether the nurse is able to get all of her work done within the allotted time frame. If she is getting it all done, she has a reasonable workload with room for additional assignments. If she is taking shortcuts to get it all done, the workload is too heavy. Unfortunately, most facility managers do not care about the workload test but instead overload the nurses to get the most nursing care for their dollar regardless of the quality of the care.

You Should Know if the nursing home mandates its employees to punch out on time. Some nursing homes have a "no overtime" policy. If your facility has such a policy, it should raise a red flag. It is rare that nurses and nursing assistants regularly leave work at the exact end of their shift; there is simply too much work to be done. Staff members operating under a no-overtime policy are often engaged in a race against the clock to finish on time. If the facility policy mandates that its employees leave promptly at the end of their shift, the management is not concerned with the quality of work being performed.

In some facilities that have a no-overtime policy, it has been my experience that, rather than risk being reprimanded by management regarding a late punch-out, the staff will neglect what still needs to be done or leave what was not done for the next shift in order to leave on time. The oncoming shift cannot be responsible for any unfinished documentation, so the departing staff often neglects it or completes it inaccurately in order to leave on time.

Most companies would rather avoid paying its employees overtime, yet in my opinion, any facility that institutes a no-overtime policy has a complete disregard for the reasons so many staff members are punching out late. It is more likely than not that the shift is already understaffed, which explains why no one can get out on time. At one such facility where I worked, I observed a few nurses and nursing assistants punch out on time but then return to the unit to finish their jobs without pay. I saw even more employees leave the facility without completing their end-of-shift duties, like emptying linen hampers, restocking supplies for the next shift, and, most important, documenting resident care.

Obviously, you want your parent in a facility that is sufficiently staffed to deliver good care. Ask the director how staffing shortages are handled at your facility. You need to determine if the people caring for you parent are doing so while constantly pressed for time.

DAY-TO-DAY NURSING HOME OPERATION

Now that you know the basic issues surrounding nursing homes, you are ready to walk through an average day in a typical facility. Again, the following description does not apply to all nursing homes but will give you a general idea of how most nursing homes carry out day-to-day business.

Most nursing homes divide their days into three eight-hour shifts. The day shift usually runs from 7 a.m. to 3 p.m., the evening shift from 3 p.m. to 11 p.m., and the night shift from 11 p.m. to 7 a.m. Many facilities have what is called a Baylor schedule, which is typically long shifts on Saturday and Sunday and no weekday hours. Some facilities utilize a twelve-hour Baylor shift model, which usually involves a change of shift at 6 a.m. and 6 p.m. or 7 a.m. and 7 p.m. To keep things simple, I will assume that your parent's facility operates on an eight-hour workday with shift changes at 7 a.m., 3 p.m., and 11 p.m.

You Should Know if your facility allows nurses to work sixteen-hour shifts. Many nurses have to work a sixteen-hour shift due to the sudden illness of a co-worker, severe weather conditions that prevent a relief nurse from traveling, or any other emergency. There are many jobs that can be performed safely for sixteen consecutive hours; however, nursing is not one of them. I have worked my share of sixteen-hour shifts (and have seen many other nurses work sixteen-hour shifts) and I can tell you from personal experience that even under optimal working conditions, it is very difficult to maintain the necessary pace and focus to deliver good care. The continuous physical and mental demands dull the abilities of even the sharpest nurses near the fifteenth hour, or even sooner in some cases. In my opinion, if a facility does not allow its nurses to work sixteen-hour shifts, then you can probably assume it is making an effort to promote a safe environment for your parent.

The first duty of the day for the staff on a typical long-term-care unit is to have all of the residents awake and out of bed for breakfast. Some residents stay in bed for breakfast and either feed themselves or wait for a staff member to feed them. The start of the nursing home workday begins at approximately 4 a.m., when the night shift bathes and dresses those residents who are qualified candidates for such an early start. The night shift begins the bathing process at this early hour to ease the burden on the day shift staff, who could not possibly bathe and dress twenty to fifty residents by the end of the morning if they were to start at the beginning of their 7 a.m. shift.

Of course, there are residents who prefer to get out of bed early. In fact, many residents complain that they are not assisted early enough, though there are relatively few requests for assistance at 4 a.m. The day shift is inundated with requests for assistance with getting dressed between 6 a.m. and 9 a.m., so the night shift is charged with easing that burden. A very common complaint among the arriving day shift employees is "Night shift only got up four/five/six residents. How are we going to have time to do so and so? We're short-staffed as usual." The more residents already up, bathed, and dressed by the time the day shift arrives, the easier the day shift's morning will be.

The same system is applied to the morning medications. The night nurse is assigned an early medication pass, which is scheduled to begin around 5 a.m. in order to relieve the day nurse of a larger medication pass. Nurses are permitted to deliver a medication due at 5 a.m. between the hours of 4 a.m. and 6 a.m., leaving a one-hour window before and after the specified time. In reality, this early medication pass starts at 4 a.m. sharp. The nurse may even change the time that a medication is due (if the physician did not specify an exact time) so that it can be given at an even earlier hour. Most medications are delivered to the residents at a time that is most convenient to the staff.

Some residents are naturally early risers and request medications as early as possible. Regrettably, others are awakened, medicated, bathed, and dressed at a very early hour simply because they are unable to object. These are typically the residents who have no family members to object on their behalf. The staff meets virtually no resistance when performing this type of "convenient" nursing care. Unfortunately, the residents who are awakened in the wee hours of the morning are usually asleep and slumped over in their chairs by the time breakfast arrives.

You Should Know if your parent is one of the residents awakened at 4 a.m. and whether he or she approves of that early morning routine or would rather get up at a later hour. If your parent is unable to articulate a description of the morning routine, perhaps you could find out for yourself by paying an early morning visit to the facility. By familiarizing yourself with the morning routine, you can determine whether your parent is comfortable with the current waking and medication schedule.

Another method the night shift employs to help the day shift (in this case, the "help" is for the nurses' convenience rather than the residents) is to awaken some residents at 4 or 5 a.m., bathe them, and leave them in bed so that when the day shift arrives they need only reawaken the residents and help them to their chairs for breakfast. The rest of the morning care is already done.

The residents that I have seen bathed, dressed, and medicated at the earliest hours are the residents who do not speak. The first residents up are usually the ones who have lost their mental faculties and are unable or unwilling to refuse. If you find that any of these early morning techniques are a part of your parent's care, and he or she would rather not be disturbed at that early hour, speak to the unit manager and insist on a new schedule.

THE 7–3 SHIFT

The day shift staff on a typical long-term-care unit of twenty-five or thirty residents usually consists of one nurse and between two and four nursing assistants. The number of nursing assistants, like the number of nurses, varies among nursing homes, although with predictable regularity, you will see that there are never enough to do what is required. The nursing assistant's job, discussed in greater detail in the second chapter, is the toughest job in the entire facility. More work is increasingly expected from an ever-shrinking number of nursing assistants.

The day nurse receives a report from the night nurse regarding any changes or events that may have occurred during the night. The change-of-shift report can be either a tape-recorded message that the night nurse made throughout his shift or a written or oral face-to-face report. If the oncoming nurse has not worked that particular shift in a while—or has never worked it—the report may be more in-depth. Conversely, if the night nurse is new or from a nursing agency, the report may be less informative. I once saw an agency nurse end her shift by reading off the list of nursing home residents: "Mrs. Smith had a good night, Mrs. Jones had a good night," even a resident who had passed away weeks ago was said to have had a good night. In this case, the list of resident names the nurse had been given at the start of her shift was not updated, and she was too busy or overwhelmed to notice it was incorrect.

The day nursing assistants pick up where the night assistants leave off, getting everyone up and dressed before breakfast, which is either delivered to the unit on a cart or served in a dining room. Usually, it is a combination of both, with some residents going to the dining room and some eating on the unit.

After the nurse has received the shift report, she pushes a medicine cart down the hall, stopping at each room and/or the dining room to deliver medication to the residents. Most residents receive between one and fifteen medications each. In my experience, the average number of medications per resident is approximately eight. Some residents receive eyedrops, medication patches, insulin injections, syrups, or inhalers in addition to their pills. The morning medication pass normally takes two to three hours to complete.

The morning is the busiest time at the nursing home because the focus is on getting everyone medicated and ready for breakfast. It is also when all the residents need to get bathed and dressed. Because each nursing assistant may have nine or more residents to assist, many residents must wait until after breakfast to get dressed for the day. Usually by 11:00 a.m. all of the residents are medicated, dressed, and their beds are made. In the following chapters, you will discover the many shortcuts that are taken in order for the staff to meet its shift-end deadlines.

It has been my continued observation that many nurses (including myself), at many facilities, are not able to complete the morning medication pass within the allotted time frame. Not only is the sheer volume of the medication to be delivered extremely heavy, but there is usually only one nurse in charge of passing the medications, delivering care to residents, speaking to family members, taking phone calls from doctors, and supervising nursing assistants. Some facilities even require the only nurse on staff to attend meetings during the shift, leaving the unit unmonitored, or monitored by a nurse on another unit.

While the nursing assistants deliver breakfast trays to the residents who choose to eat in their rooms, the residents who are at risk for choking are encouraged to eat in the dining room so that they can be monitored. After everyone who can eat independently has been served their breakfast, the nursing assistants and, in some facilities, the nurse, feed the residents who cannot feed themselves.

Residents who need to be fed usually sit in a separate section of the dining room; however, some residents who need assistance are fed in bed because they are very difficult to get out of bed. For example, if a particular resident requires a mechanical lift or the assistance of two people to get her up, the staff may leave her in bed to save time during mealtime rushes. The problem with this arrangement is that residents are often unable to eat at an angle that is conducive to swallowing safely. I have seen countless residents being fed their meals while their heads were raised only slightly, leaving them vulnerable to choking or aspirating. Even when the head of the bed is completely raised, many residents slide down the mattress so that they are eating in a very awkward position.

Another problem for residents who eat in their beds is that by the time the breakfast trays are passed out and the staff has time to feed the residents who need help, their food is cold, and they must eat it alone. The residents in the dining room are usually fed first, then the staff return to the unit to feed the residents who are waiting to be fed in their rooms.

Quite often, staff members feed more than one resident at a time since there are usually more people that need feeding than there is available staff to feed them. It takes a long time to feed all of the residents their entire meals, which is why often only part of the meal is fed to each resident. If a resident eats extremely slowly, he may not have a chance to eat the entire meal. Your parent should be eating a full meal, he should choose where he eats, and he should not be left in his room for meals just because it requires extra effort to get him out of bed.

Breakfast is usually completed by 10 a.m., and the race to get everyone bathed and dressed is resumed. The nursing assistants move quickly in order to finish dressing their group of residents before lunch. After everyone has been dressed for the day, the nursing assistants continue to answer the call lights, assist residents to the bathroom, and clean residents who are incontinent throughout the day. The residents are transported to their appointments inside and outside of the building. Some residents attend bingo games or other activities. The focus then turns to lunch.

The nurse turns her attention to the treatment of wounds, documentation, checking blood sugar levels of the diabetic residents, and assessing new complaints of pain or injury. During the morning medication pass, it is common for at least one of the residents to experience an episode of chest pain, a fall, or a new illness that requires assessment, monitoring, and additional documentation. This is also the time for the nurse to attend any care plan meetings that may be scheduled.

Care plan meetings are federally mandated meetings designed to improve the quality of care for nursing home residents by identifying care issues and implementing a preventive or corrective plan for treatment. Nursing homes that accept payment under the Medicare or Medicaid agreement are bound by this requirement. The meetings are held every month or quarter and are normally attended by the resident and one nursing home employee from each discipline involved in the resident's care. For example, representatives from dining services, rehabilitation, nursing, and social services gather together to discuss the current plan of care for the resident. The resident's family is usually encouraged to attend in person, but a conference call can be arranged, if necessary.

This is the best forum for you to ask questions and offer suggestions regarding all aspects of your parent's care. Everything from food preferences to medication changes is discussed. The meeting usually lasts fifteen to thirty minutes, and most facilities are flexible about scheduling the meeting according to the availability of family members.

You Should Know that care plan meetings that include the resident's family member or medical power of attorney (MPOA) last longer and accomplish more of the resident's goals than those at which a family member or other legal representative is not present. The alert and oriented resident almost always has some complaints or comments about the way care is delivered. The complaints are often "My call bell is not answered very quickly and I cannot get to the bathroom in time." "There are never enough staff members on duty." And "They are always sending me the food I don't like." In my opinion, when the staff is accountable to a family member for finding a solution to these complaints, greater results are achieved than when the staff is accountable only to the resident.

I have seen these meetings last only five minutes when the resident or the resident's family is not present. I have seen meetings conducted without the resident present, even though he or she would have understood what was being discussed. You should review any documentation that was generated during these care plan meetings if you are unable to attend. Arrange to have another family member attend in your absence, if possible.

By the time lunch arrives, the residents have been bathed, dressed, and medicated. Many have attended an activity such as church, bingo, bowling, or exercise class. The activities vary from facility to facility. Hair appointments and naps are also common activities for late morning. Residents who are able to navigate independently go in and out of their rooms at their leisure, while others need assistance to go to the bathroom and to their beds for naps. Many residents are incapable of knowing when they are wet from urine, so the nursing assistants are responsible for periodically checking them.

The residents who are not capable of moving themselves around in their wheelchairs and beds rely on the nursing assistants to routinely reposition them. By late morning, most of the immobile residents should have been repositioned at least once. Not only is frequent repositioning a comfort issue for the resident, it helps to prevent skin breakdown and bedsores, which are a major threat to nursing home residents who are immobile. Such sores occur when there is a constant, uninterrupted pressure on the skin, usually over a bony area. Bedsores are often the result of lying or sitting in the same position for too long. Most facilities try to follow a timetable of every two hours for repositioning residents. There is usually a "check-the-box" form for the nursing assistants to complete after such residents are repositioned.

Before and after lunch, therapists see the residents who are in need of any type of rehabilitation. This applies particularly to the skilled-care residents who normally see one or more therapists on a daily basis. The podiatrist often makes rounds during the day shift, seeing all of the residents who have been referred for issues of the feet. The dentist and the medical doctor also see residents at some point during their designated day.

Lunch is served in the same manner as breakfast. A large food cart is pushed down the hall, and the nursing assistants deliver the meals to those residents who do not go to the dining room. Residents who cannot feed themselves are fed by the staff. Lunch is somewhat different from other meals in that there are more staff members in the building, and many participate in helping to feed the residents. At more than one facility, I have seen the administrator regularly help feed residents. Secretaries, social workers, and family members often feed residents during the lunch period. Because the lunch meal normally has the greatest number of helpers, visiting only at lunchtime will not give you a clear picture of how all of the meals are delivered and fed to the residents.

The nursing assistants are extremely rushed after lunch, as their duties include getting many residents dry and into bed for their afternoon nap. The nursing assistants again take residents to the bathroom and reposition those who cannot move themselves. They typically start at one end of the hall and work their way to the other end, making sure everyone has been helped to the bathroom. At this time, the nursing assistants have yet to complete all of their paperwork and much is expected of them in terms of documentation. They must chart weights, meals, snacks, and activities for each resident, as well as empty the linen hampers and trash bags, clean the unit, and give a verbal report to the nurse about the care of their residents.

There is usually a group activity after lunch, such as a movie or a game. Some facilities have regular bus trips or visiting entertainers. Afternoon snacks are usually offered, especially to the diabetic and underweight residents.

The nurse has a second round of medications to pass out, although the afternoon pass is not nearly as heavy as the morning medication pass. This is because most residents take the bulk of their prescribed medication in the morning. Residents who are scheduled to receive medications in the afternoon will usually get them delivered at the same time so that the nurse can pass out all of the afternoon medications at one time. At some of the busier nursing homes, the total time a nurse spends actually passing out medications during her eight-hour shift can surpass five hours.

Wound treatments are done in the afternoon if the nurse was unable to do them before lunch, which is usually the case. New medications are ordered from the pharmacy, the medication cart is restocked, appointments for the residents are made, and new orders from the doctor are transcribed. Recommendations from therapists are documented and the medical assessments are charted. It is during the afternoon that the day nurse must document everything that she has done during her shift. The presumptive motto in the nursing profession is "If it wasn't documented, it wasn't done." Everything must be documented.

You Should Know that the nurse's notes should include a description of everything that has been done for your parent that day, including documentation of complaints, behavioral changes, medication changes, new symptoms (such as vomiting, headache, diarrhea, or sore throat), bruises, and the status of any medical equipment, such as tubes or catheters. For skilled-care residents, a more frequent, in-depth assessment is charted. The notes should be like a diary of everything that has occurred with your parent. Each entry describes how care was delivered, who delivered it, and how it was tolerated by the resident. The doctor often refers to these notes to determine if the current medical plan of treatment is appropriate.

Your parent has access to these notes at any time. You have access to these notes if your parent has authorized you to have such access or if you are his or her legal representative. If you want to be kept abreast of all that is happening with your parent, regularly reading these notes is one way to keep updated. You need only ask the unit manager for copies of the notes.

Understand that the nurses are trained to document their entries in a facility-friendly fashion. For example, if the wrong medication is given to a resident, the nurse does not need to write "Mrs. Doe was accidentally given 40 mg. of Lasix at 9:00 a.m., a medication that was intended for another resident. The doctor was notified of the error. A Medication Error Form was completed and delivered to the director of nurses per facility protocol." Nurses are instead advised to write something like "Mrs. Doe received 40mg. of Lasix at 9:00 a.m. The doctor was notified, no new orders."

The fact that an error occurred does not need to be written in the nurse's notes. Additionally, facility administrators do not want nurses to indicate in their documentation that additional forms were completed after an incident, thereby drawing attention to documents that may later be part of an investigation. In other words, your parent's medical chart does not include all of the documentation that may have been generated following an unusual occurrence. Some documentation regarding daily care may even be recorded on forms that are not part of the medical record.

Medication error forms, incident report forms, wound notification forms, weight charts, food and fluid intake records, and many infection-control documents are kept separately from the medical record. Sometimes these forms are kept in another location because the names of several residents appear on one document. Other times, the facility uses the forms for investigative purposes, or they may not want the forms to be readily accessible by the resident or her representatives.

Nursing homes have become increasingly document-sensitive due to the many abuse and neglect claims against them. For any area of nursing care that, if neglected, could lead to a lawsuit against the facility, a form has been created. For instance, many unsteady residents wear alarms on their chairs that beep loudly when the resident stands up, alerting the staff to a potentially injurious situation. Many residents have fallen despite having the alarms in place because the battery was dead or the unit was not turned on.

There is now a form for the nursing assistants to complete after they have checked that the alarm is in place and functional. Usually this form is completed every four hours or every shift. Often the nurse has a form for the exact same purpose, which *she* signs, indicating that the nursing assistants have completed *their* forms. This system of double documentation is designed to ensure that after the nurses have overseen the work of the nursing assistants, the task was unquestionably completed. Many of the same events that are documented by the nursing assistants are documented by the nurse, as well.

The problem with this system is that often the information documented by the nursing assistants conflicts with the documentation completed by the nurses. This is so because there is always so much paperwork to be done that most of it is done in a hurry, leaving plenty of opportunity for error.

There is a form to be completed after the delivery of a snack to a resident, since weight loss can be a sign of neglect. There are forms for documenting the size and consistency of each resident's bowel movement, how much urine was excreted, the percentage of each meal eaten, the amount of fluid consumed, attendance at exercise groups, participation in group activities, temperature and blood pressure, unusual occurrences, departure from the facility with family or friends, shower or bath, condition of skin, location of hearing aids during the day and night, and many other seemingly mundane acts. The nurse and nursing assistants must complete these forms at various points during the shift.

THE 3–11 SHIFT

The shift changes at 3:00 p.m. Some facilities require that staff members of both the oncoming shift and the departing shift walk the unit together as part of their shift change report. This gives the oncoming shift a chance to make sure all of the residents are present and doing well and to check for cleanliness before accepting the unit.

The evening shift is not usually staffed as well as the day shift, but, like the day shift, the evening shift has the responsibility of checking to make sure all residents are kept dry during their shift. Residents tend to spend more time in their rooms in the evening, so the nursing assistants try to get to each room every two hours. Often there simply is not enough staff to accomplish the task, and residents remain in the same position for long periods of time.

Before and after dinner, which is served between 4:30 and 6:00 p.m., the nursing assistants get the residents into their bedclothes and ready for bed. Some facilities have policies that prevent nursing assistants from getting anyone dressed for bed before dinner, especially those residents who eat in the dining room. Some residents request that they be prepared for bed before dinner so that they don't have to wait for assistance after dinner; however, in the interest of promoting residents' right to privacy and dignity, they are not dressed in their bedclothes and then taken to the public areas of the facility, such as the dining room.

In every nursing home I have visited, this rule is ignored. The rule is ignored because the low number of evening staff requires the bathing process to be started early. And, typically, the residents dressed for bed ahead of schedule and taken to the dining room in their nightclothes are the ones who are unable to realize the difference or unable to voice opposition.

If they are not scheduled for a bath, residents are helped to the sink in their room for a short bath before getting dressed for bed. Every resident has a scheduled bath day: usually one bath or shower a week. If the shift happens to be short-staffed in the evening, which happens often, baths or showers are often canceled, and a resident might go up to two weeks or more without a proper bath or shower. The other shifts try to make up for previously canceled baths and showers, but more often than not, they are unable to pick up any extra duties.

You Should Know how many baths per week your parent receives and whether he or she is comfortable with the current bath schedule. You should know when your parent's scheduled bath/shower day is and if it is frequently canceled. When the facility is understaffed, the first shortcut is usually canceling baths. This occurs most frequently on the evening shift and on weekends. Some facilities do not even schedule baths on weekends due to anticipated staffing shortages.

You should also know that some nursing homes will, upon request, allow for two baths or showers per week. I have seen family members request such a schedule for their parent, and, when possible, the nursing home will comply. You will probably have better luck getting two baths scheduled if at least one is scheduled during the day. If your parent is scheduled for two weekly baths, his or her chances of getting at least one bath per week will be greater.

Before dinner, the nurse checks the blood sugar levels of the diabetic residents and administers insulin and other medications. She usually helps to pass out the meal trays and feed residents. Residents are then transported from the dining room back to their rooms or to a common area. Sometimes, there is a movie after dinner in a common area where the residents can congregate.

While the nursing assistants race to get everyone put to bed, the nurse races to give everyone their evening pills before they are in bed. Evening treatments for wound and skin care are done. Snacks are supposed to be passed out between 7:00 and 9:00 p.m. Usually all of the residents have been medicated and are in bed by 9 p.m.

The evening shift has documentation responsibilities similar to that of the day shift. Everything the staff has done and observed must be documented. The end-of-shift duties such as cleaning, restocking supplies, and laundry are the same for the evening shift. The nursing assistants continue to answer call bells and respond to chair and bed alarms that go off when an unsteady resident stands up alone.

THE 11–7 SHIFT

The third shift arrives at 11:00 p.m. Although it might not seem like the third shift would be all that busy, it certainly can be due to the fact that it is often barely staffed. The third shift has the task of repeatedly turning the residents from side to side in their beds, checking for wetness, and answering call bells. The assumption might be that all of the residents sleep through the entire night, but many are up frequently and need assistance. At 4:00 or 5:00 a.m., the cycle is repeated.

On weekends, the routine can vary somewhat. Some facilities have more and better activities on the weekends, while others have no activities at all. Depending on your facility, some variation of this typical cycle will be the routine. You now know how the average nursing home operates.

CHAPTER 2

NURSING HOME STAFF

"I don't go out on the floor. I'm afraid of what I might see."
—nursing home administrator

In this chapter I will tell you about the employees you will likely find at most nursing homes. I will describe their jobs to help you better understand who is responsible for each aspect of your parent's care. Some nursing homes have eliminated positions in an effort to cut costs; however, you will find that most of the positions mentioned here exist under a different title, or it might be that one person is filling two positions. Often, a position exists but is temporarily vacant. When you know which employees are responsible for which activities, you will have a better sense of whom to contact when you have a concern.

In chapter 8 you will find a fill-in-the-blank chart in which you can keep track of the names, titles, and telephone numbers of the nursing home employees you may need to contact. I advise you to become friendly with as many people on the chart as possible and to use a pencil when listing the employees because the names will change often.

As I stated in the introduction, I feel that having a loved one in a nursing home is like having a second job. This chapter will tell you all you need to know about your "co-workers" and which ones to approach for each issue related to your parent's care.

MANAGEMENT STAFF

Nursing Home Administrator

The nursing home administrator is responsible for everything that happens within the facility. She is responsible for the budget, staffing, quality of care, and ensuring that the facility is in compliance with state and federal regulations. In essence, she is responsible for the daily operations of the entire facility. The administrator does not personally oversee all activity within the facility but has several people below her to assist with the management of operations in each department.

Some administrators are highly visible, easily approachable, and actively involved in the care of the residents. They may know the staff members and residents by name and can often be seen on the nursing units assisting with resident care. Other administrators, unfortunately, are secluded in a separate wing of the facility and rarely interact with the nursing staff or the residents and their families. Regardless of which management style they employ, administrators have the most power to implement change. If you have a concern or a suggestion regarding your parent's care that is not addressed at the lower level, this is the person you should contact.

Medical Director

Long-term-care facilities must provide medical care in accordance with state and federal regulations. The medical director is the physician in charge of ensuring that all medical care delivered within the facility is in compliance with all regulations. Often the facility's medical director is the primary care physician who treats the residents of the facility, but this individual may also supervise the medical care without actually treating residents at the facility. He may or may not have an office within the facility.

In theory, the medical director determines which medical policies and procedures the facility should adopt. While some medical directors are extremely involved in the oversight of medical care, it has been my observation that many medical directors rely on the director of nurses to ensure that the facility is operating within the boundaries of the regulations.

Nursing Home Physician

Some facilities have a group of doctors who see the residents on rotating shifts, taking turns covering nights and weekends for emergencies. Others have only one doctor who visits the facility on specified days of the week, once a week or even less often. The doctor typically visits the nursing home to see each resident every sixty days (or whatever the law mandates in your parent's case, usually every thirty or sixty days).

A list of residents who are "due" to be seen by the doctor is generated, and the doctor visits each resident on the list. Sadly, I once heard a doctor tell a resident who wanted a doctor visit, "I can't see you today. Medicaid won't pay for it because I just saw you last week." While true, the doctor's statement was heartbreaking because the resident did not understand the rules governing doctor visits.

In addition to seeing residents in order to satisfy the thirty- or sixty-day requirement, the doctor might also see a resident the nurse has asked her to see. If a resident has had an injury or a recent change in his or her condition but is not on the list, the nurse may ask the doctor to see that resident. Still, much of the care that a nursing home doctor delivers is via a telephone call with the nurses who call the doctor after hours and on weekends. If a doctor has recently treated a resident over the telephone, that resident will also usually make it onto the doctor's next list.

It is also common for the facility to employ a nurse practitioner, either as an assistant to the physician or to regularly see the residents and report to the doctor any new illnesses or injuries. While it is possible for your parent to continue care with the physician she had prior to entering the nursing home, most residents transfer from their primary care physician to the nursing home physician.

Under some circumstances, it is to the benefit of the resident to continue the relationship she has with her own doctor instead of switching her care to the nursing home doctor. For example, I have seen some residents unhappy with the infrequent number of visits that the nursing home doctor makes to the facility. Many independent residents who are capable of maintaining their relationship with their primary care physician do so in order to see their doctor when *they* choose rather than seeing the doctor according to the schedule of the nursing home. Also, many residents are uncomfortable transferring years of history with their own doctor to a doctor they do not know.

It may be possible to transfer a parent's care to the facility physician upon admission to the nursing home while at the same time maintain a relationship with the primary care physician in the event hospitalization is required. Most nursing home doctors do not have hospital privileges, so nursing home residents are treated by a new and different physician each time they are transferred to the hospital.

Common complaints I have heard from residents who transfer their entire care to the nursing home physician are "I do not want to wait until Tuesday when Dr. Doe comes to visit" or "What does she know? She's not my doctor!" Such complaints may come from residents who were not involved with the decision to transfer care or who do not remember taking part in the decision. Usually, such complaints come from residents who transfer their care without knowing how many times a week or a month they will actually be able to see their new doctor.

Most residents do not realize that the facility doctor can be contacted at any time. Twenty-four hours a day, seven days a week, a facility doctor is available by telephone. The doctor on-call may not be the primary doctor of the resident, but a covering doctor is always available. Of course, it's not a good idea to make a habit of having the doctor contacted in the evening hours or on weekends, but if you think there is a medical emergency with your parent and the staff is reluctant to make the call, you should insist on notification.

If your parent wants to maintain a relationship with his current doctor rather than switch to the nursing home doctor, it is important to find out if the current doctor will agree to treat your parent once he becomes a nursing home resident. Some doctors simply do not treat nursing home residents; some will see residents only in their office. Additionally, you must learn whether your parent will need transportation to and from appointments and what will happen if he is unable to travel to the office.

If your parent expects to remain under the care of a doctor outside of the nursing home, you should find out what on-call coverage is provided when that physician is not available. If the coverage is limited to weekdays, I would recommend transferring care to the facility physician.

You Should Know that the nursing home doctor (or primary care doctor treating your parent) can write an order for almost anything your parent needs. For example, when the nurse delivers medication to the resident, the nurse is required to stay with the resident until the medication is swallowed. Some residents request that the nurse leave the medication so the resident can take it at her convenience. The doctor can write an order stating that the nurse "may leave medication at bedside." Of course, the resident must be capable of taking her medication without assistance or supervision, or the doctor will not write the order.

Some residents like to keep over-the-counter medications such as Tylenol or ibuprofen in their rooms. I have seen residents have their TUMS antacid tablets taken away because, even though it is an over-the-counter medication, it must be administered by a nurse according to most facility policies. If the family, the resident, or the nurse requests that the doctor write an order allowing the medication to be left at bedside, the request is usually granted.

Another area where I frequently see a doctor's order for practical intervention is with regard to eating in the dining room. Most nursing home managers prefer that everyone eat in the dining room rather than allowing residents to eat in their rooms where there is no one to help should a choking emergency arise. If your parent prefers to eat alone in his room—and is not at risk for choking—the doctor can write an order stating that he be able to do so.

Whether your request is for salt, dandruff shampoo, a heating pad, or an evening cocktail, almost any special request can be granted with permission from the doctor, providing your parent exhibits the degree of independence required.

Director of Nurses

The director of nurses, almost always a registered nurse, is in charge of hiring and supervising every nurse and nursing assistant in the facility. She oversees the daily operations of the nursing units. She is responsible for ensuring that the nurses and nursing assistants are properly trained and delivering quality care according to the policies of the facility. She prepares the nursing home for state inspections, ensures that the facility is in compliance with state and federal regulations, and implements a plan of corrective action if the nursing home is found to be out of compliance. She reviews accident reports and conducts investigations regarding resident injuries and/or resident mistreatment.

The director is required by law to report certain injuries and deaths or suspected resident mistreatment to the state agency that oversees nursing home care. In many instances, the director has the authority to decide whether a particular injury necessitates state agency involvement. In my opinion, this flexible reporting procedure grants nursing home management far too much discretion. The injuries that require state agency involvement and the possible interpretations of this legal statute are discussed in chapter 4.

The director is usually on duty Monday through Friday. Her primary role is supervisory, but often she is involved in actual nursing care to the extent that it enables her to ensure that the residents are receiving adequate care. At some facilities, she is utilized as a staff nurse in situations when there are not enough nurses to work on the units.

Many nursing homes are continually hiring and training new staff because of the high turnover. The director position is no exception. I know of a few facilities that have employed three nursing directors in a one-year period, each one staying only a few months!

Assistant Director of Nurses

The assistant director of nurses, often, but not always, a registered nurse, takes the place of the director of nurses in her absence. His primary duties involve assisting the director of nurses and usually include oversight of the nursing schedule and training programs. Both the director of nurses and the assistant director of nurses supervise the nurses and the nursing assistants in their daily routine of delivering care to the residents.

At smaller facilities, the director of nurses (DON) and the assistant director of nurses (ADON) take turns being the on-call supervisor for nursing or staffing issues and emergencies that occur after hours and on weekends. Their responsibilities vary from facility to facility. The DON and the ADON should be able to answer any of your questions regarding your parent's medical care, care plan, medications, treatment schedule, and any other direct-care issues.

Unit Manager

The unit manager is typically a registered nurse but can be a licensed nurse or, in some cases, a nonmedical person. Her responsibility is to ensure that everything on her unit is operating according to the policies of the facility. She supervises the staff on her unit and conducts evaluations of their performance. She should be familiar with all of the residents on her unit. She may participate in meetings with residents and family members. In some smaller facilities, if licensed to do so, she may pass out medications to cover for nurses who call in sick. She is typically on the unit Monday through Friday.

You Should Know the unit manager well because she may be the only member of the medical management team who sees your parent on a regular basis. Because of staffing rotations, the use of temporary staff, and the high staff turnover rate in many nursing homes, the unit manager might be the only regular member your parent has on her health care team. Many staff nurses work on different units each day, but the unit manager is more likely to be on the same unit every day.

While it is likely that the nurses you talk to regarding your parent will be familiar with his or her individual care needs, for better continuity of care—and to ensure that you are not talking to new ears each time you want to address an issue—it is best if you direct as much of your communication as possible to the unit manager. Concerns you have regarding your parent's care that have not been resolved after speaking with the unit manager should be brought to the attention of the director of nurses.

Admission Coordinator

The admission coordinator is sometimes a nurse but is not required to be medically trained. He handles the admission paperwork and orients the new resident to his or her new home. Since many residents are admitted to a hospital before being admitted to the nursing home, he often visits prospective residents in their hospital rooms to prepare them for their nursing home admission.

He is responsible for learning what medical, psychological, and physical needs the new resident will have once in the nursing home and for relaying that information to the facility management staff. Because the nursing home must be able to meet each resident's individual needs, the management staff as a group usually determines whether the facility can meet the resident's needs and, subsequently, whether to accept the resident.

You Should Know that your parent may fare better if his or her admission to the nursing home takes place at the beginning of the week. When a resident is moved to a nursing home, even on a temporary basis, there are many services that need to be set in motion. A resident's admission involves the participation of almost every discipline within the facility, including therapy, dietary, and nursing. It usually takes a few days to work out all the kinks that are not immediately apparent when a resident is initially admitted to the facility, and, to complicate matters, the department heads are typically unavailable on weekends.

If your parent is admitted on a Friday and discovers that she wants a change in diet, a new mattress, a different walking cane, or to implement any other seemingly simple change, she may have to wait until Monday to request a resolution. Also, getting the telephone and television hooked up may not be possible on a Friday afternoon.

Many nursing homes will allow a resident to be admitted on a weekend, a transition that almost never goes smoothly. Weekends are when nursing homes are the most understaffed. If your parent is moving from her home to the nursing home, you can usually choose on which day the move will occur. If your parent is being admitted under emergent circumstances or if she is being discharged from a hospital to the nursing home, you may have no choice in the matter since hospitals and insurance companies are not as flexible as they once were regarding the number of allowable days per hospital stay and the date of discharge. However, if it is possible to give yourself the cushion of a few weekdays, I recommend doing so.

Social Worker

The social worker is usually not a nurse but certainly can be at some facilities. Typically, a bachelor's degree is required to hold this position. You will often find that a facility has a director of social services along with one to three social workers on staff. Some facilities have just one full- or part-time social worker, depending on the size of the facility. Larger facilities (one hundred and twenty or more residents) are required to employ at least one full-time social worker.

The social worker is involved with admissions to the nursing home and acts as a resident's advocate to obtain all the services he may require. She has a vast knowledge of the area agencies and the services each has to offer. She also assists the family in understanding the financial complexities involved with nursing home living. She sometimes acts as a buffer between the resident and all of the other disciplines.

The social worker is what I call the "problem solver." She can find a solution to almost any challenge that may confront a resident (except the understaffing issue). I have seen social workers solve roommate disputes, financial difficulties for family members, staff and resident personality conflicts, and noise complaints. You can bring any problem or concern related to your parent's nursing home stay to the social worker, and if she cannot personally solve your problem, she can direct you to someone who can.

MDS Nurse

The minimum data set (MDS) is a compilation of data about each resident that is sent to the Centers for Medicare and Medicaid Services (CMS) and used for financial reimbursement. The nursing home must supply this information to prove that the resident actually needs the services and assistance for which the government provides funds to the facility. The information is also used for public quality-of-care information and statistics.

The minimum data set nurse, or MDS coordinator, a registered nurse, is responsible for reporting this extensive and in-depth information on government-prepared forms to CMS. The specific care each resident requires from nursing home staff is documented on the MDS forms. Information such as the resident's ability to turn independently in a chair or in bed; how much assistance is required for eating, dressing, and bathing; mood and behavior issues; and medications is included on these forms. Everything that is done for a resident and everything the resident can do independently is documented on the MDS forms.

The MDS coordinator is usually not a hands-on clinical nurse and quite often is not personally familiar with the residents. She usually obtains the information she needs to complete the forms from the nursing assistants or nurses or directly from their paperwork. Some facilities do not employ a full-time MDS nurse but rather require that the staff nurses complete the MDS forms.

Infection-Control Nurse

This position is usually held by a registered nurse. She monitors all of the residents in the facility with infections and those at risk for developing an infection. She reviews the residents' medical charts and conducts educational training for employees to ensure that the facility remains in compliance with infection-control policies. If you have a concern regarding whether two or more residents should be sharing a room due to possible communicable diseases, this nurse can help you.

You might think that nursing homes function at a level of proficient awareness that would prevent a resident with an infectious disease from being placed in the same room as a resident with a compromised immune system (and therefore unable to fight off an infection), but you would be mistaken. It happens quite frequently.

For certain infectious diseases, regulations require that a sign be placed on the door referring potential visitors to the nurse's station before entering. You will probably not be told by the staff that your parent's roommate has an infection. Due to the laws that protect the health information of each resident, you will not know that your parent is being exposed to a potentially dangerous germ. If you notice that a new sign has been taped to your parent's door detouring visitors to the nursing station, you know that there is some new health condition that may affect visitors.

You should know that if your parent has a roommate, the possibility for cross contamination exists. If you see a sign placed outside your parent's door, and your parent is not the one with the infection, you need to make an inquiry as to what infection your parent's roommate has contracted. You may not get as much information as you would like about the medical condition of your parent's roommate due to privacy laws; however, you can learn a great deal by simply being observant. Listening to the conversations of the caregivers will probably give you information about a resident's infection. Also, you can ask the caregivers who come into the room, especially if you've befriended them. Caregivers at the top of the management chain are less likely to dole out protected information than those with their sleeves rolled up, doing the dirty work.

You will almost certainly need to remind caregivers to wash their hands before they touch your parent. They have so much work to do in such a short amount of time, one of the most frequent shortcuts is failure to wash hands between caring for residents.

Know that the mere presence of a sign outside the door may not indicate an infectious disease. (The use of oxygen often requires a sign.) If there is a sign on the door, and the staff members are wearing masks and/or gowns upon entering the room, a resident likely has an infectious disease.

FRONTLINE NURSING HOME STAFF

Wound or Treatment Nurse

Residents get wounds from injuries when they fall and, because their skin is so thin and fragile, from rubbing against a door or wheelchair with even a slight amount of force. A common type of wound treated by the wound nurse is a pressure sore or bedsore. These sores usually occur over bony areas like the heel, coccyx (tailbone), or any area of the back.

The treatment nurse inspects and treats all wounds and implements skin care regimens for all residents in the facility. She does not typically have any more nursing education than the staff nurses, but if she has been in this position for any length of time, she has (hopefully) gained some insight into the newest procedures for proper wound and skin treatment.

Many facilities have eliminated the position of treatment nurse and instead have the staff nurse incorporate wound treatments into her routine. A wound is usually measured and a record of each measurement is kept in the resident's chart. In my opinion, it is best if the facility employs a full-time treatment nurse or, alternatively, has the same nurse or nurses regularly treating the wounds, so they can notice changes in size, color, and drainage of the wounds.

I should alert you to the fact that I have worked in facilities that employed a treatment nurse and/or a staff nurse treating wounds, yet many wounds still increased in size because the nurse deviated from the standard wound protocol. If your parent has a wound, insist on viewing the wound record, which will indicate the growth or recession of the wound size. Have the record explained to you if it is not legible. Also insist that the dietitian be consulted if applicable, because diet plays a large role in wound healing.

You Should Know that some facilities have access to a wound specialist. This is the person the facility contracts with for advice on treatment measures for wounds that are not healing with standard treatment protocol. He may be an employee of the pharmacy, another nursing home, or an area doctor's office. His sole professional mission is treating wounds. You should ask the director of nurses whom the facility consults with as a wound specialist. If your parent has or develops an open wound, particularly a bedsore, it is imperative that appropriate treatment measures start as soon as possible. Such wounds are painful and can lead to infection and decreased quality of life. Insist that the wound specialist be consulted.

I have seen facility staff try numerous wound-healing creams, foams, and bandages that are ineffective, yet the staff remains reluctant to contact the designated wound specialist, even as the wound gets larger. I have seen numerous nurses who are not specialists in wound care suggest treatment after treatment and take several courses of action that yield no sign of improvement before asking the doctor for a wound consult. Meanwhile, the wound worsens. You should know that the doctor often (not always) listens to the suggestions of the nurses and prescribes according to their suggestions. It is best to have the wound consultant brought in sooner rather than later.

You should also know that when the medication nurse is assigned the additional duty of wound treatments, the treatments may not always get done. The only time both medication duties and wound treatment duties should fall to the same nurse is when the workload is manageable enough to ensure that both tasks can be completed without taking shortcuts. I cannot tell you how many times my shift ended before I had time to do the treatments. I had to either wait until my relief nurse arrived and do them then or ask the next nurse to do the treatments that were supposed to be done during my shift.

Many nursing homes require the nurse to put the date and her initials on the bandage after each wound dressing is changed. I have removed many, many bandages from wounds that were ordered to be changed daily that had dates up to two weeks old. I have also found bandaged wounds on residents who were never reported to have a wound requiring treatment. In such cases there was no follow-up care from the time the wound was first bandaged because the other nurses never knew that a wound existed.

If your parent gets a wound, you should do five things. One, you should personally make sure the doctor looks at the wound regularly. Two, you should know the frequency of the dressing changes and make sure the wound is being changed as often as ordered. Three, you need to monitor the progress yourself by either frequently looking at the wound itself (preferred) or the documentation. Do not be afraid to take pictures each week. Sometimes, taking pictures of the wound is part of the facility's wound-management program. Four, you must insist that the doctor write an order for a consultation with the wound specialist if the wound is not superficial. (Professional consultations do not occur without a written order from the doctor.) Fifth, to avoid creating more pressure to the area, be absolutely certain that the staff is keeping the affected area clear. They should be repositioning your parent at least every two hours.

Sometimes the wound specialist recommends a pressure-relieving mattress, which the facility may or may not have in the building. The director of nurses should be able to help you get one if it is recommended.

Registered/Licensed Nurse

These two types of nurses usually occupy the position of staff or floor nurse. The significant difference between a registered nurse (RN) and a licensed practical nurse (LPN) or licensed vocational nurse (LVN) is that the RN has completed at least one more year of education. Both can fill the position of a regular staff nurse, sometimes known as the medication nurse. This nurse spends most of her day passing out medication to the residents.

The medication nurse might work on a regular floor each day or she might "float," or rotate to other floors or units to meet the needs of the facility. It is my opinion that when nursing homes staff the same nurse with the same residents, better care is delivered. The less time the nurses spend getting to know the residents and their routines, the more time they can devote to delivering care. Many facilities have full-time nurses, part-time nurses, per diem nurses (who work only when they are asked and are usually without a weekly commitment), and agency nurses.

Agency Nurse

An agency nurse is employed by an agency not affiliated with the nursing home. He is a temporary employee intended to supplement the nursing home staff when needed. The facility usually notifies the agency of its staffing shortages, and the agency sends nurses to the facility on designated days, either at an appointed time or at a moment's notice. Agency nurses work only the days they choose to work and are not typically entitled to benefits like health insurance and vacation pay. The facility pays the agency a handsome hourly rate, and from this the agency takes its share and then pays the nurse. In most cases, agency nurses earn more money than the regular staff nurses of the nursing home because the agency charges such a high rate to the facility.

Some facilities refuse to hire agency nurses and boast of being "agency-free," while other facilities are so understaffed they must routinely rely on agency nurses and nursing assistants to cover several positions each day. Nursing homes typically have difficulty maintaining a regular nursing staff and must resort to some creative techniques of staffing their facilities. For instance, agency-free facilities must use their management nurses as medication nurses when shortages leave them desperate for nurses, or they may offer bonuses to their regular staff for accepting extra shifts.

You Should Know how often your facility uses agency staffing because it is an indicator of the continuity of care being provided at the facility. Common sense would dictate that you would rather have your parent treated by staff members who know her well and respect her needs. While some facilities who hire agency nurses book the same nurses repeatedly, this may not always be possible. Some agency nurses will work one shift in a nursing home and then get sent to another facility the next day, or they may decide that they are not going back to a particular facility if the workload was too heavy. Agency nurses have the option of choosing the facilities in which they will work. If a facility uses agency staffing, it is possible for your parent to have a new nurse several times a week.

In my own experience as an agency nurse, I refused to return to a few nursing homes because the work expected of the nurses created an environment that was extremely unsafe. At one facility, I refused to accept an assignment that included caring for over sixty residents. It was a unit that was normally staffed with two nurses, but one nurse had called in sick and the facility wanted me to accept the entire unit "just until they found someone to come in."

At another facility, the assignment was heavy and made worse by the fact that all of the people on duty that evening, including all three of the nursing assistants, were agency staff and none of us were familiar with the residents. I quickly learned to tell my agency, who wanted to book me for several shifts in advance, that I would go to a new facility once and, after working that shift, decide if I would accept more shifts.

When a new staff nurse is hired at a facility, she usually works side by side with another staff nurse for one or two weeks before being scheduled on her own. A first-time agency nurse is somehow expected to jump right in and assume the role of seasoned employee. One night, as an agency nurse, I was expected to train and orient a new nurse the facility had just hired. I had only been to the facility a few times myself. What kind of training could the facility possibly expect this new nurse to receive from someone who had very little knowledge of the facility and the residents?

Agency staffing can be a lifesaver to the nursing home. When I finally found a few nursing homes that I liked, my agency booked me there regularly for months at a time and everyone benefited. The residents were treated by the same nurse on a consistent basis, and I was able to learn each of their likes and dislikes. I did not have to experience a "first day on the job" over and over again, and the nursing home was consistently staffed.

Knowing if a nursing home uses agency nurses and nursing assistants can help you determine if your parent is getting the continuity and level of care that all residents need but that agency staff are not always able to provide. By the same token, if your facility is agency-free, you should know whether it is simply running below the optimum staffing levels or whether the facility has found a creative staffing alternative.

Some facilities will go agency-free for a time and then revert to using agency staff frequently. You could ask the director of nurses if her facility is using agency nurses; however, you should be aware that a "no" in December might change to a "yes" in March. To determine the agency staffing situation for yourself, simply look at the name tags of the nurses and nursing assistants. Both agency staff and regular staff are required by law to wear name tags. The regular nursing home staff name tags will show the name of the nursing home, whereas the agency name tags will indicate the name of the agency. Another way to determine if your facility is understaffed is to check the classified section of the local newspaper to see if the facility is running ads on a regular basis. You can check most newspapers online.

Medication Nursing Assistant

Medication nursing assistants (MNAs) or medication licensed nursing assistants (MLNAs) are licensed nursing assistants who have completed an additional course of study beyond their nursing assistant training, usually several weeks in length, which teaches them about medication administration. MNAs are not nurses, but they assume some of the responsibility of passing out the medication, thereby theoretically freeing the nurse to complete other tasks.

Unfortunately, in some facilities, MNAs are used to replace a nurse rather than assist a nurse. For example, if a facility has four wings and each requires one nurse, a facility might staff two wings with nurses and two wings with MNAs. MNAs are required to be supervised by a nurse and cannot perform many tasks that are reserved for an RN or an LPN/LVN, such as taking a medication order from a doctor, giving injections, wound assessment and treatment, and skilled documentation.

In those cases where the facility uses an MNA to replace a nurse, the nurse responsible for supervising the MNA must do the work of two nurses to compensate. If an MNA is covering one unit and a nurse is covering the other unit, the nurse must leave her unit and go to the MNA's unit to do her injections, doctor's orders, documentation, and all other tasks that the MNA is not legally permitted to perform.

The MNA earns more per hour than a nursing assistant but much less of an hourly wage than a nurse, so nursing homes that employ MNAs instead of nurses for medication administration save money. The controversial question is whether the facilities are misusing the MNAs.

I have worked in a few facilities that use MNAs, and in my experience, my workload increased because the facility was using an MNA in place of a nurse. If I was the supervisor of the MNA, I had to do my work and much of hers. If I worked the shift directly following the MNA, I found that the end-of-shift report reflected the basic level permitted by her scope of practice. I often found that residents had complaints or injuries that were not properly assessed during the previous eight hours because the MNA did not realize that certain signs and symptoms needed further probing.

Nursing homes will claim that their use of MNAs is due to a nursing shortage, but such hiring practices often create more work for existing nurses and lead to their resignation, thereby perpetuating the perceived shortage. Why would a nurse work at a facility where she must perform her own duties as well as the duties of an MNA? Many nurses feel that they have enough work on their hands without the added responsibility of running to the MNA's unit each time there is a crisis she is not equipped to handle.

Other major concerns are whether the MNAs are properly supervised during their shift and who ultimately shoulders the responsibility for the safety of the residents on the MNA's unit. The level of supervision over an MNA will vary from nursing home to nursing home. Some facilities interpret "supervision" to mean that a nurse must be in the building, while others interpret it to mean that a nurse must be available by telephone. Is the MNA responsible for the safety of the residents on her unit or is that the duty of the nurse on a nearby unit? I have heard many nurses voice concern over whether the utilization of MNAs is a safe practice due to the many ambiguities surrounding their job description.

In my opinion, many factors play a role in determining whether the facility safely utilizes the MNA, including whether the MNA knows the residents well, how long she has been a nursing assistant, how much work is delegated to the MNA by the nurse, and the proximity of the nurse to the MNA. The best assignment for an MNA is to supplement the existing nursing staff while avoiding additional staffing hazards.

Nurse's Aide/Licensed Nursing Assistant

Nurse's aides or licensed nursing assistants are the backbone of all nursing homes. They are the hardest-working and lowest-paid members of the nursing staff. They are the closest people to your parent. They wash, dress, and bathe all of the residents and help them use the toilet.

They have a difficult and often unpleasant job. When a resident has bowel incontinence, the nursing assistant must wash fecal material out of the clothing, because the laundry department cannot accept laundry soiled in this manner. They clean feces and urine off the floor to make it ready for the housekeeper to clean. They must clean stool and urine from residents' body creases several times a day. They endure all sorts of offensive odors, take out the trash, and clean the residents' rooms and the kitchen area. They are the primary caregivers of the residents. They have the most to do in the least amount of time of all the nursing home employees. It has been my continued observation that this position is always extremely understaffed.

You Should Know the nursing assistant-to-resident ratio because this is the most telling piece of information you can possess regarding the quality of care at your facility. During each shift, the residents on the unit are divided among the nursing assistants on duty. If the unit has sixty residents and six nursing assistants, each nursing assistant cares for ten residents. The fewer residents a nursing assistant has, the more time she has to devote to each resident. I believe that this is the area of nursing home care with the most room for improvement, since most nursing assistants cannot possibly do the job that is expected of them within the allotted time frame.

Often the nursing assistants have seven, eight, nine, or even more residents in their care. It is a difficult and time-consuming task to bathe, dress, and help to the toilet such a large number of residents each morning, and it is tough, backbreaking work. Most of the residents require assistance to the toilet several times each shift and help to bed for a nap at least once during the shift. Additional duties aside from resident care include heavy documentation responsibilities and various cleaning jobs. I have heard the same complaints in almost every facility I have worked at or visited: "I don't know how they expect us to get everyone done." "There are too many residents on my list." "Mrs. Smith is only getting a quick wash; I just don't have time to give her a proper bath." "It's almost 9:30 and I still have four residents left on my list."

I have seen over and over the many shortcuts that nursing assistants must take to care for everyone on their list. Oral care and shaving are frequently skipped; cleaning under the fingernails is rarely done; morning, afternoon, and evening snacks are not delivered; and meals are fed to the residents quickly or not completely finished. Crust around residents' eyes is often not cleaned because morning care is so abbreviated it may only consist of a wet cloth to the face before getting dressed.

Many nursing assistants take shorter breaks or skip their breaks entirely. At the end of the shift, their documentation is either skipped, rushed through, or inaccurately done. Jobs like lifting a completely immobile resident, which requires two nursing assistants and/or a mechanical lift, are often attempted or completed by only one person in an effort to save time. This practice often leads to injury of the nursing assistant or the resident.

Nursing assistants are also responsible for answering the call bells that the residents ring when they need something. They are constantly being interrupted from helping one resident to answer a bell from another. It is simply not the case that a nursing assistant works with one resident until he is done and then moves on to the next resident. If a nursing assistant steps out of a resident's room and into the hall to fetch a sheet or a towel, he is often immediately asked to go help with another task. This is because so much of resident care requires two people.

It is common to see nursing assistants working double shifts. So few of them are scheduled to work each shift that when one calls in sick (which is a frequent occurrence), the facility usually asks a nursing assistant from the previous shift to stay for another shift. Nursing assistants have a high rate of job-related injuries, which further complicates the staffing situation. The turnover rate is so high, it can be dizzying. It is understandable that nursing assistants frequently leave jobs and move on to facilities that promise better pay and better staff-to-resident ratios.

Nursing homes are notoriously understaffed for several reasons. The first and most obvious reason is that the facility is trying to cut financial corners by staffing as few employees as possible. Second, the facilities set their own optimum staffing levels. The facility managers decide how many nursing assistants should be on duty during each shift to adequately care for all the residents. The number is always too low. The people who decide how many nursing assistants it takes to care for a group of residents have not invested the time it takes to accurately make that determination. Once the determination is made, they allow the facility to operate with staffing levels below the optimum levels that they have set!

Because facilities are staffed with so few nursing assistants, it is a sad but true fact that when a resident wants help to clean out her closet, write a letter, or go outside for some sunlight, the nursing staff rarely has time to oblige. They often have time for only the most basic and necessary requests. When some residents are waiting up to forty-five minutes to be taken to the bathroom, nursing assistants are not able to help residents with such nonurgent tasks.

It is not that the nursing assistants do not want to do their work thoroughly; there simply are not enough nursing assistants to adequately care for a given number of residents. I know of a nurse who would not accept her nursing assignment until she learned how many nursing assistants would be with her on her shift. If the number was too low, she would call the director of nurses and give her the opportunity to remedy the shortage before she refused to work.

In my opinion, a nursing assistant should have no more than six residents requiring moderate to maximum assistance. This is not a ratio you will find in most facilities, but it should be. In such a scenario, the resident would get sufficient care and the call bells would be answered in a timely fashion. The documentation would be more reflective of the care actually delivered, and the number of work-related injuries and resignations would be minimal.

The nursing assistants typically know your parent better than the other staff do because they have the most contact with the residents. They know if your parent is wearing her brace or if she is taking it off during the day, or whether she is doing her exercises, wearing her special hose, or interacting with other residents. They know if her stools are loose or if she is constipated, exactly what she is eating, what her mood is, and whether she has any physical complaints.

Agency Nursing Assistants

Agency nursing assistants are contracted to work in the nursing home in the same manner as agency nurses. They are sometimes semiregular and come to the facility five days a week, if they find a facility they like working in and it suits the needs of the facility. However, when a facility gets different nursing assistants every day, the residents have a new employee taking care of them each day. Again, you will be able to identify agency employees by their name tags when you visit the facility.

Private-Duty Nursing Assistants

A private-duty nursing assistant is usually hired by the family when the resident requires or desires more assistance than the nursing home staff is able to provide. He works in the nursing home, but solely for the one resident he was hired to assist. Typically, this happens when a resident is extremely limited in what she can do for herself. I have seen families rely on this service during the rehabilitative stages after an injury or surgery or at the end-of-life stages.

The private-duty staff is essentially agency staff. Most nursing agencies have employees who are available for private hire to the general public. Agency staff can provide one-on-one care in the nursing home or at a private family home. Nursing homes do not generally provide one-on-one care to residents except for very brief periods of time. They do not typically staff well enough under ordinary circumstances, so you can imagine how difficult it would be to provide one-on-one care.

Feeding Assistants

Many facility managers have recognized what a monumental task it is to feed every resident each meal with a limited number of nursing assistants. To eliminate some of the pressure on the nursing assistants at mealtimes, the position of feeding assistant was created. The feeding assistant must take a short course before she can begin properly feeding residents. The course teaches the feeding assistant to recognize chewing and swallowing difficulties and also summarizes what to do in a choking emergency.

CONSULT STAFF

Speech Therapist

The speech therapist may be an employee of the facility or he may be independently contracted to treat residents at your nursing home. He works with residents who have difficulty swallowing or speaking. Difficulty of this type can be the result of a stroke, an injury, or a general decline in health. For a resident to receive speech therapy, the treating physician must write an order for these services. The therapy session usually ranges from two or three times a week to several times a day and can continue for several weeks or even months.

The speech therapist makes recommendations to the doctor about consistency of food and fluids and whether a resident should eat independently or with supervision or assistance. Documentation of the therapy visits are recorded in the resident's medical chart by the therapist. The family should be updated regarding any changes in a resident's method of eating and drinking.

One of the most common recommendations from the therapist is for a resident to have thickened fluids because the resident is unable to swallow fluids at the normal consistency. To thicken the fluids, a powder thickener is stirred into the resident's drink, and within minutes, the drink becomes as thick as honey, or thicker, depending on the order. This order is common for stroke victims.

I have seen several residents who were supposed to be given thickened liquids choke after they were given fluids of a normal consistency because the staff was unaware of the order. This happens frequently with agency staff. If your parent has this order in place, you may wish to remind staff members of it.

Occupational Therapist

The occupational therapist, like the speech therapist, is either an employee of the nursing home or is hired under contract from another facility or agency. She works with residents who have difficulty using their hands and arms due to stroke, multiple sclerosis, injury, arthritis, or general decline in health. She often helps residents to relearn how to bathe and groom themselves.

Physical Therapist

Many facilities either have a physical therapist on staff or have contracted with one to make regular visits. The physical therapist works with residents who have a fracture, chronic pain, or arthritis, usually in the leg or hip, or who have difficulty walking or balancing. The therapist teaches the resident to balance, exercise, walk with her new injury, and maneuver up and down stairs with crutches, a cane, or a cast. They practice a few times each week until the resident becomes independent or his or her condition stabilizes. The goal for any resident in therapy is to restore function, increase strength, and improve mobility.

Podiatrist

At many facilities, a podiatrist makes monthly visits. She cuts toenails; examines skin, tissue, calluses, and bunions; and is sometimes involved with treatment of wounds on the feet. In some nursing homes, the podiatrist has minimal involvement with the care of residents' feet, and the nurses or nursing assistants are charged with trimming the residents' toenails.

If your parent is a diabetic (whose lower legs and feet should be regularly evaluated), you should ask the unit manager or director of nurses about the frequency of podiatry visits and suggest that your parent be put on the list to see the podiatrist at each visit. If there is no visiting podiatrist, do not trust that the nursing home staff will regularly and adequately examine your parent's feet and toenails.

In most nursing homes, the visiting podiatrist receives a list from the nursing staff indicating which residents are in need of foot or toenail care. Often, no particular person is assigned the task of ensuring that residents in need of podiatry services get added to the list, and the task is given a low priority. It is possible for many residents to fall through the cracks and not be seen by a podiatrist for several months.

Dentist

I know of nursing homes that have a dentist come to the facility to see residents and others that send the resident to the dentist's office. Again, there is often an irregular and unreliable system for making sure all residents get appropriate dental care. Almost all residents experience problems with their teeth or dentures at some point during their nursing home stay. Also, all residents should be on a program for regular cleanings and/or checkups.

Ophthalmologist

The eye doctor is another professional not usually found on the nursing home staff but is one whose visits are important for all residents. Regular eye exams are not scheduled for many nursing home residents unless they exhibit problems or are already being seen by an ophthalmologist when they enter the nursing home.

You Should Know whether your facility has contracts for podiatry, dental, and ophthalmology services to determine whether your parent will receive any of these specialized treatments. You should know the frequency of such doctors' visits to the facility and the procedure for obtaining their services. Some facilities have such poor coordination with these outside services that, in some instances, I would recommend that you contact them directly and bypass facility involvement altogether.

First, find out if the podiatrist and dentist come to the facility on a regular basis. Some eye doctors and dentists are unable to treat residents in the nursing home because the equipment they need to conduct their examination is not mobile. There should be a system in place for the facility staff to recognize a resident's need for services and a procedure by which those services are obtained. Find out whether the required professional service is available to the resident in the nursing home or if the resident needs to visit the office.

Once you know the procedures used by your facility for obtaining each of the services, determine if they are functional. In a facility where the podiatrist visited each month, I saw residents with toenails so long their ability to walk properly was affected. No one had taken the necessary steps to ensure a podiatry visit for those residents.

I spoke with a visiting dentist who stated that during his examination of most residents, it was apparent to him that the most basic oral care, like brushing the teeth, was not being done. I agree with him. I once attempted to give a resident her morning medications, but the resident would not open her mouth. I was finally able to coax her into allowing me to look inside her mouth, where there was a piece of meat from the previous evening's meal. It would have been impossible for this resident to have had any type of oral care before she went to bed.

Ask the unit manager if your parent is going to see a dentist, podiatrist, and ophthalmologist regularly or only when he or she exhibits a need for such services. If the service is provided only when someone on the nursing home staff notices that your parent has a need, ask to have appointments automatically scheduled monthly or annually, depending on the service and your parent's particular needs.

ANCILLARY NURSING HOME STAFF

Director of Activities

The director of activities is responsible for planning events that will occupy and entertain the residents. At some facilities the director of activities works alone, while at others, she has a staff of two, three, or more activity assistants. They arrange church services and have dancers, singers, grade-school children, and magicians come to perform for the residents. They also schedule bus trips, shopping trips, bingo games, exercise groups, movies, and quilt-making classes.

Some nursing homes have a large recreation department that can offer exciting activities to keep the residents constantly involved and socially interactive, while other nursing homes regularly park everyone in front of a television set. Most nursing homes provide a calendar of events, which outlines the activities that will be scheduled on each day of the month.

You Should Know what activities have occurred over the last few months and ask to see recent activity calendars so you will know how committed the facility is to providing a social environment for the residents. Ask if any of the activities on recent calendars were cancelled. Some facility recreational programs look better on paper than they do in actuality.

You should check to see if the activities are primarily scheduled during the day or if some events are scheduled for the evening. You should know what shifts the activity department staff works. If the staff works mostly weekdays, you know that not much happens for the residents during the evenings and on weekends because the nursing staff generally does not arrange social activities. Ask if all of the activities are inside the building or whether the residents get to go out as a group. You should know if the activity department has a van or a bus to transport residents. If not, you will know that all of the activities occur within the building or on the nursing home property.

Director of Food Services

The director of food services is responsible for providing adequate nutrition to all of the residents. This position may be held by a registered dietitian, but that title is not a requirement. There are usually several people employed under the food service director who work in the kitchen performing cooking and cleaning tasks.

A "fill-in-the-blank" menu is often provided by the kitchen staff for the residents to indicate their meal preferences for the following day or upcoming week. The level of help that each resident receives to complete the menu varies from facility to facility. Some nursing homes have an employee of the food services department who regularly visits each resident to help the resident complete the menu. Other facilities deliver the menu to the resident, and if it is not completed, no effort is made to determine the resident's preferences.

You Should Know what food items were listed on the menus during the previous few months to determine whether the meals have adequate variety and appeal. One of the most common complaints that I have heard from the residents regarding the facility food is that the same meals are served over and over or that the food is lousy in general. I know of a few nursing homes that serve lobster or steak every few months, and the residents enjoy those occasional special meals. Other nursing homes seem to have an endless supply of fish sticks and hot dogs on a menu that simply repeats itself each week.

You should ask if the kitchen staff can provide hamburgers or grilled cheese sandwiches if a resident does not like the menu on a particular night. Many nursing homes offer two choices, and if a resident does not like either of those choices, a peanut butter and jelly sandwich is offered.

You should also know that you can make special requests of the kitchen staff. For instance, if your parent has chronic constipation, ask for prune juice or some sort of fibrous cereal with each breakfast. If he has a sweet tooth, ask for two deserts with the evening meal. If he likes eggs, ask that eggs be served instead of pancakes each morning. The meal can be tailored to a resident's liking to a great extent.

You should also schedule a few of your visits at mealtimes. Request to have a meal with your parent. There is usually a small fee for a guest meal, but you will get an idea of what the meals are like and whether you want to make any future requests for your parent.

Director of Housekeeping/Laundry

The director of housekeeping and laundry is responsible for keeping the facility clean and supplied with fresh sheets and towels. There are usually several housekeeping employees on duty during the day and few, if any, on duty during the evening hours. The laundry department is also in charge of washing residents' clothing and returning it to their rooms.

Many facilities offer residents and their families the option of having their laundry done at the facility or taking it home to wash. Most residents and families prefer to have their laundry done by the facility since it is far more convenient. However, given the large volume of laundry done by the housekeeping staff, special attention is not usually devoted to items such as wool sweaters or delicate blouses.

You Should Know that everything you bring into the facility should have your parent's name on it to prevent it from being lost. All clothing should be labeled with a permanent felt-tip pen or have a name label sewn into the fabric. The laundry personnel are often left to guess which resident owns an unlabeled clothing item. The laundry staff also finds unlabeled jewelry, hearing aids, and dentures in the sheets and clothing.

Labeling should not be limited to clothing. It is a good idea to label eyeglasses, hearing aids, dentures, books, wigs, quilts, and anything else you do not want to replace. Some items may require engraving. For especially valuable items, consider taking a photograph that you can use to show the staff in case it is misplaced. Remember, confused residents often wander into other residents' rooms and take things that look similar to things they once owned.

At most nursing homes, there is a pile of unlabeled glasses that no one is able to match to a particular resident. Many of the nursing home staff members will attempt to make their own taped-on labels, which never seem to last. A common question is "Don't these look like Helen's glasses?" A common response is "Yeah, I think so. Try them on her."

Director of Maintenance

The maintenance director and his staff are responsible for repairs and maintenance of the building, its fixtures, and many appliances. Often, their job includes repairing toilets, wheelchairs, beds, and televisions. At many facilities, someone in the maintenance department must approve any electronic equipment you bring for your parent before it will be allowed in his or her room so they can inspect the cords for safety. Occasionally, maintenance staff will do minor repair work on residents' personal equipment.

Beautician

The beautician usually has a shop within the facility, and residents' appointments are typically scheduled weekly. Sometimes she comes to the rooms of residents who are unable to make the trip to her shop. The fees and variety of services offered at the beauty shop vary from facility to facility.

Seamstress

The seamstress labels clothing with the resident's name and also performs clothing alterations. Unfortunately, I have seen many nursing homes eliminate the position of seamstress due to budget cuts. In some cases, nurses and nursing assistants will take residents' clothing home to label or repair on their own time.

Volunteers

Not all nursing homes use volunteers. In my opinion, a nursing home should not operate without volunteers. They account for so much of the meaningful work that gets done when regular staff is too busy. Volunteers often work at the information desk or assist to transport residents to and from activities and appointments. They also pass out mail; assist residents with opening, reading, and responding to their mail; and visit residents who would otherwise have no company.

You Should Know that becoming a volunteer in your prospective nursing home, or in the nursing home where your parent already lives, is the best way to learn about your nursing home. While in this volunteer position, you can see for yourself what type of care your parent is receiving. You can meet residents and learn what they like and dislike about the facility. If you cannot personally volunteer, have someone do it for you, like a family member or a friend.

CHAPTER 3

RESIDENTS' RIGHTS

"I don't have enough staff to babysit her.
She needs to be medicated."
—a statement made by many nursing home nurses who medicate
overactive residents because there is not enough staff to closely
monitor everyone

In 1987 the federal government approved the Nursing Home Reform Act in response to public concern over the poor quality of care the elderly were receiving in nursing homes across the country. The new law provided rights to all nursing home residents and required facilities who accept payment from Medicare and Medicaid to abide by these rules, which were designed to improve the quality of care for nursing home residents.

The law created a set of rights for each and every nursing home resident and required nursing homes to operate under specific guidelines. The portion of the act that gave residents clear, enumerated entitlements was aptly named the Resident's Bill of Rights. These rights dictate how residents shall be treated once admitted to a nursing home. On the wall of every nursing home, you should see the Residents' Bill of Rights posted for all to see.

The formal source of these rights, which are actually laws, is the Code of Federal Regulations (CFR), Title 42–Public Health, Part 483, Requirements for States and Long-Term-Care Facilities. To better understand the application of these laws, I divided them into two sections. I list the rights of the residents in chapter 3 and the responsibilities of the nursing home in chapter 4. If a regulation indicated that it was an entitlement of the resident, it is listed in chapter 3. If a regulation required the facility to take specific action, it is included in chapter 4.

I did not include every regulation that pertains to the rights of residents and the responsibilities of nursing homes because I do not believe that every regulation is being violated. My intention with chapters 3 and 4 is to familiarize you with those regulations that I believe are frequently violated or have the potential to be easily violated.

The list of regulations that you will likely see posted in every nursing home is similar to this basic summary of the rights afforded every resident:

§483.10. *The resident has a right to a dignified existence, self-determination, and communication with and access to persons and services inside and outside the facility. A facility must protect and promote the rights of each resident, including each of the following rights:*

- To exercise his/her rights as a resident of the facility and as a United States citizen;
- To be informed of his/her rights and responsibilities;
- To manage his/her financial affairs;
- To choose a personal attending physician and participate in planning treatment;
- To personal privacy and confidentiality;
- To voice grievances without reprisal and have the facility respond to those grievances;
- To examine survey results and any plan of correction;
- To refuse to perform services for the facility;
- To privacy in written communications;
- To visit with relatives and other visitors;
- To the use of a telephone where calls can be made without being overheard;
- To retain and use personal possessions, unless to do so would infringe upon the rights of others;
- To share a room with his/her spouse if both consent to the arrangement;

- To self-administer drugs if determined that this practice is safe; and
- To refuse a room transfer from a distinct part of the institution to another distinct part.

At first glance, this posting appears to illustrate that the facility is making a solid, personal commitment to each resident. But remember, these laws were devised in response to public outrage over poor care, and all nursing homes are required to post these rights. The implementation of the new laws improved nursing home care in many areas, but twenty years later, the quality of nursing home care remains far from satisfactory. The rights are often not adhered to because most facilities do not always staff adequately enough to provide the level of care the law requires. As long as nursing home managers continue to follow the current trend of inadequately staffing their facilities, the bulk of these rights will continue to be much less of a guarantee than the legislature intended.

In addition to the Bill of Rights, which is only a small portion of the Nursing Home Reform Act, the new law created several other explicit entitlements for nursing home residents. Most facilities do not post, or explain to the residents, the pages and pages of laws that expound upon the basic rights, nor do they detail every regulation in its entirety. Before I introduce the legal entitlements not covered in the basic Bill of Rights, let's take a closer look at these Residents' Rights.

RESIDENTS' RIGHTS

§483.10(a)(1). *The resident has the right to exercise his/her rights as a resident of the facility and as a citizen of the United States.*

Your parent has the right to exercise any of his or her rights that have been granted under the Nursing Home Reform Act. He or she may exercise his or her voting rights and any other rights granted as a United States citizen or resident.

You Should Know that many residents decline to pursue their basic entitlements under the Nursing Home Reform Act because they are acutely aware of the likelihood of an unfavorable outcome should they attempt to seek enforcement. Many residents try to avoid being forceful or seen as a "troublemaker" because they must live with the staff members every day, and they would rather preserve, not jeopardize, these relationships. Residents know that there is very little anonymity in the complaint process and that filing a complaint could destroy the relationship between the resident and the caregivers.

Understandably, residents do not make requests they know will be ignored, and residents who are oriented to their surroundings are aware of the root of most problems: understaffing. Numerous residents have told me that they have voiced grievances regarding the continued low staffing but were told "there is no room in the budget for additional staff" or "there is nothing that can be done when people call in sick." In light of these excuses, residents learn that it is futile to complain.

§483.10(b)(1). *The facility must inform the resident both orally and in writing in a language that the resident understands of his or her rights and all rules and regulations governing resident conduct and responsibilities during the stay at the facility.*

Your parent must be given a verbal and written description of the rights, receipt of which must be acknowledged in writing prior to or upon admission to the facility. Any amendments made to the rights must also be given to your parent in writing.

You Should Know that nursing home nurses do not give a thorough verbal explanation of the rights upon admission to the facility. Usually an abridged version of the basic fifteen rights is quickly handed to the resident, buried in multiple pages of other admission paperwork. (The admission process is no exception to the hurried fashion in which nursing home business is conducted.)

§483.10(c)(1). *The resident has a right to manage his or her financial affairs, and the facility may not require residents to deposit their personal funds with the facility.*

Your parent has the right to manage his or her own money or to appoint someone to manage the money on his or her behalf. Your parent cannot be forced to entrust personal funds to the nursing home.

§483.10(d)(1). *The resident has the right to choose a personal attending physician.*

Your parent can choose to keep his own doctor, transfer to the facility doctor, or select a new doctor. He can switch doctors at any time, even after admission to the facility, so long as the accepting physician is willing to take him as a patient. The facility is required to assist your parent in reaching this decision.

It is my opinion that residents and their families are often steered into choosing the facility doctor because it is more convenient for the facility if all of the nursing home residents are seen by its doctor. It is easier for the staff to coordinate legally required physician visits for each resident if only the facility doctors are involved in the process.

You Should Know whether your parent is satisfied with his or her doctor. Your parent may not be aware of her right to request a different physician. I worked at two nursing homes where nearly half the residents at each facility repeatedly complained that they did not like the facility physician. One of the facilities replaced the doctor in question, while the other facility did not. Nursing home managers rarely address the issue of a resident who is dissatisfied with a particular physician unless there are numerous complaints.

§483.10(d)(2). *The resident has the right to be fully informed in advance about care and treatment and of any changes in that care or treatment that may affect the resident's well-being.*

This regulation requires the nursing home staff to tell your parent (or designated legal representative) about his or her condition and course of treatment before it is initiated.

Typically, nursing home medical care is delivered by the doctor visiting the residents on their scheduled "doctor day." The prospective medical treatments are discussed between the resident and the doctor and then implemented accordingly.

If the resident is not capable of understanding or discussing potential treatments, the doctor will order specific treatments or medications and relay those orders to the nurse, who in turn notifies the family or other representative. Some facilities have a reliable, efficient system in place for family notification, while others consistently fail to notify the residents' family members about new treatment orders.

Another way medical treatment can be implemented without prior notification to the resident or resident's family is when the doctor is notified by telephone that a particular treatment is not working or that there is a new condition that needs intervention before the doctor's next visit. In this case, a nurse accepts a treatment order over the phone from the doctor and, for any number of reasons, does not inform the resident or the family before ordering the medication or treatment. The nurse may have been too busy to telephone the family, or, if it was late at night, the message to telephone the family in the morning was misplaced.

§483.10(d)(3). *The resident has the right to, unless adjudged incompetent or otherwise found to be incapacitated under the laws of the State, participate in planning care and treatment or changes in care and treatment.*

This regulation requires care providers to actively include your parent in the planning of her care. Every change in your parent's plan of treatment should be the result of a discussion about her goals and options. No treatment should ever come as a surprise to a resident or the resident's family.

Every nursing home resident who is able to understand her health status should know the name and purpose of each medication she is taking. Still, I medicated hundreds of lucid nursing home residents who asked me why they were taking a certain medication. If a resident is not able to understand her medical condition, her legal representative should know the name and purpose of each of the resident's medications.

Quite often residents ask, "Who decided I should be taking this?" or "I never took this before I came here, why do I have to take it now?" Some residents easily forget what they were told about their treatment plan, others were told too quickly or the information was skimmed over during a brief meeting with the doctor. Unfortunately, many residents have never had their medications explained to them.

§483.10(e). *The resident has the right to personal privacy and confidentiality of his or her personal and clinical records.*

Your parent is entitled to privacy when he receives visitors and when he receives treatment from the doctor, nurse, or nursing assistants.

You Should Know that it is common practice for residents to receive medications, injections, and treatments in the most populated areas of the nursing home, in plain view of other residents and visitors. This is because the residents are often gathered in common rooms at the same time. It would be impossible for the staff to meet medication deadlines if each resident were moved to a private room each time a medication was given.

It can be embarrassing for residents with swallowing difficulties to take medication in front of others, especially if the medication must be crushed, mixed in ice cream or applesauce, or hand-fed. The most common way this regulation is violated is when a staff member approaches a resident who is seated with other residents and family members and announces, "It's time for me to check your blood sugar" or "It's time for your wound treatment."

Another frequent violation of the right to privacy occurs when a resident is being bathed either in the shower room or in his own room. Staff members who are not involved in the bathing process frequently come in to get supplies, to leave or pick up a menu, or to ask the resident a question, all while the resident is undressed. If your parent is able to verbalize his care routine, inquire as to whether he feels comfortable with the level of privacy received during care.

§483.10(f)(1). *The resident has the right to voice grievances without discrimination or reprisal.*

Your parent has a right to report inferior nursing care, habitually rude staff members, extended waiting periods for assistance to the bathroom, and any other unsatisfactory conditions without fear that he or she will receive reduced care or other discrimination because of the complaint.

A nursing home is a difficult place to live for an unhappy resident. A resident may be afraid to speak up because she does not want to be known as a complainer among the people who provide her care. Many residents have told me they feel uncomfortable reporting that a particular nursing assistant is not treating them properly. They were concerned that their care would get worse because the nursing assistant would definitely know which resident complained.

In a nursing home, it is difficult to make a complaint and have it resolved without the offenders becoming aware of who made it. However, I witnessed family members who were certain that a particular staff member was too rough or disrespectful successfully demand that that employee not be allowed to care for their parent. When this happens, the facility declares a "personality conflict" between the resident and the employee and then arranges the employee's schedule so that he or she does not work with that resident.

§483.10(f)(2). *The resident has the right to prompt efforts by the facility to resolve grievances the resident may have, including those with respect to the behavior of other residents.*

This law requires the facility to put forth a genuine effort to listen to the complaints of the residents and to try to find immediate solutions. If your parent states that her call bell is not answered promptly, that she is having problems with a roommate, or that there are never enough staff members to make sure she is taken to the bathroom before an accident occurs, the facility is required to quickly find an acceptable solution to the problem.

Throughout my nursing home experience, I heard residents complain about almost every aspect of nursing home life, including food quality, room temperature, low staffing levels, noise, violent behavior of other residents, boredom, missing clothes, and uncomfortable shoes. Most complaints, however, involve not being assisted in a timely fashion—the result of understaffing. Complaints that can be resolved easily, like a missing item, usually receive prompt attention, but since most complaints are care-related, they often go unaddressed.

Facilities do not typically increase staffing levels based on complaints from residents that there is not enough staff. In my experience, facilities boost their staffing levels in two situations. First, a facility usually temporarily boosts staffing levels in preparation for a state inspection and, second, when faced with threats of fines after failing a state inspection.

Nursing assistants are usually honest with the residents about the reason they are unable to answer their call bells in a timely manner or bring them a snack: "We are very short-staffed today." However, most facility managers tell the staff not to tell the residents that the facility is understaffed. The nursing assistants are put in the awkward position of absorbing the blame without revealing the true cause of the poor care.

§483.10(g)(1). *The resident has the right to examine the results of the most recent survey of the facility conducted by Federal or State surveyors and any plan of correction in effect with respect to the facility.*

This regulation requires the facility to make the results of recent inspections available for the residents to review. Most nursing homes display the results of these inspections near the entryway of the facility. I have also seen the inspection results made into book format, available for review upon request.

Residents, however, often do not know when these results have become available. The residents of the facility do not often enter and exit the building and would therefore not see anything displayed in the lobby. If residents do leave the building, they usually use the exit located closest to their room, which may not be the main entrance. If the results are not displayed in an accessible and obvious location, ask the administrator to show you and your parent the results. Ask the administrator to also post future results in a location that is convenient for the residents, such as the activity or dining room.

§483.10(h)(1). *The resident has the right to refuse to perform services for the facility.*

Your parent cannot be forced to perform work for the facility. Many facilities offer volunteer positions for residents who choose to perform various services, but the residents cannot be required to do any work they do not want to perform. Some of these volunteer (or paid) positions include delivering newspapers, staffing the information desk, or running errands for staff.

In my experience, residents who perform volunteer services for the facility immensely enjoy their jobs and add needed exercise and socialization to their daily routines.

§483.10(i). *The resident has the right to privacy in written communications.*

Your parent has the right to send and promptly receive unopened mail. Usually the secretary at the front office of the nursing home collects the outgoing mail and delivers it to the postmaster. Incoming mail is typically delivered to residents' rooms.

Some facilities are too busy and too understaffed to *promptly* deliver the mail to the residents. I have been to facilities where the mail is received but not delivered for several days.

§483.10(j)(1). *The resident has the right and the facility must provide immediate access to any resident by the following:*

- any representative of the State
- the resident's individual physician
- the State long-term-care ombudsman

- immediate family members
- (with reasonable restrictions) others who are visiting with the resident's consent

The facility may not prevent residents from visiting with individuals with whom the resident agrees to see; however, the facility may prevent late-night visits in the resident's room if the resident has a roommate who would be disturbed. Any visitor who provides health, social, legal, or other services to the resident cannot be refused access to the resident so long as the resident agrees to the visit.

The facility may not place visiting hour restrictions on immediate family members who are visiting the resident with the resident's permission unless such visits infringe upon the rights of other residents. In such a case, the facility must provide another private visiting area.

§483.10(k). *The resident has the right to have reasonable access to the use of a telephone where calls can be made without being overheard.*

The facility must provide a telephone for your parent to use for private calls or provide a telephone jack in his or her room.

Most facilities provide jacks in each room, and the residents pay for individual telephone service. For residents who do not purchase private service, some facilities provide a cordless telephone that is kept at the nurse's station and brought to residents' rooms as needed. There is usually an inconvenient wait for the facility telephone.

You Should Know the telephone availability for you parent. If you install a telephone in your parent's room, be sure it is a cordless phone. It is too easy for a resident to fall if he has to scramble to get to a ringing telephone. A cordless or cell phone can be easily carried from room to room within the building.

Also, you should register the number with the National Do Not Call Registry, because telemarketers incessantly call these private residential numbers despite the fact that the residents live in a nursing home.

§483.10(l). *The resident has the right to retain and use personal posses-sions, including some furnishings, and appropriate clothing, as space permits, unless to do so would infringe upon the rights or health and safety of other residents.*

Residents have a right to bring their own clothing, furniture, and other possessions as personal space permits. This regulation was designed to allow each resident to feel at home in the facility.

§483.10(m). *The resident has the right to share a room with his or her spouse when married residents live in the same facility and both spouses con-sent to the arrangement.*

This regulation prevents the facility from assigning married couples separate rooms if both spouses agree to share a room. As long as the facility is certified to provide the services that both spouses require, the facility must allow the arrangement.

§483.10(n). *An individual resident may self-administer drugs if the inter-disciplinary team has determined that this practice is safe.*

This regulation requires nursing homes to allow residents the option to store and administer their own medications. The resident must be able to do so safely as determined by the facility's health care team.

§483.10(o). *An individual has the right to refuse a transfer to another room within the institution, if the purpose of the transfer is to relocate a res-ident of a SNF from the distinct part of the institution that is a SNF to a part of the institution that is not a SNF, or a resident of a NF from the dis-tinct part of the institution that is a NF to a distinct part of the institution that is a SNF.*

This regulation gives residents the right to refuse room transfers from one section of the building, Skilled-Nursing Facility, to another section, the Nursing Facility, which delivers a different level of care.

❖

You have just reviewed the most commonly posted Residents' Rights, which are likely to be found on most nursing home bulletin boards. There are, however, additional rights that are not always displayed on every nursing home wall. All nursing home residents should be aware of every available entitlement.

QUALITY OF LIFE

§483.15(e)(1). *The resident has the right to reside and receive services in the facility with reasonable accommodation of individual needs and preferences except when the health or safety of the resident or other residents would be endangered.*

If your parent wants to stay up late, eat dessert before a meal, sleep with shoes on, take a shower instead of a bath, or makes any other request that does not interfere with the rights of other residents, his request will be honored.

Unfortunately, I have seen residents have their desserts taken away as punishment for not eating their meal. I have heard nursing assistants tell residents, "If you don't eat your meal, you won't get your dessert" as if they were scolding children. I once saw a resident have her movie taken away because it contained adult language and scenes.

I have also seen residents dissatisfied with their roommate because one wanted to sleep with the light on and the other wanted complete darkness. Rather than bring the issue to the attention of the social worker or director of nurses, the staff simply turned off the light and said, "I'm sorry, Mrs. Jones, Mrs. Smith cannot sleep with the light on."

RIGHT TO ACCESS MEDICAL RECORDS

§483.10(b)(2)(i). *The resident or his/her legal representative has the right, upon oral or written request, to access all records which pertain to* *him/herself, including current clinical records within 24 hours (excluding weekends and holidays).*

The resident or her legal representative can request orally or in writing to examine health care, financial, and contractual records that pertain to the resident, and the facility must comply within twenty-four hours, excluding weekends and holidays. The resident or her legal representative may obtain copies of such records at a fee not to exceed the community standard. The facility must comply with a request for copies of records within two working days.

You Should Know that if you regularly obtain and store copies of your parent's medical records, you will be able to help your parent in two ways. First, residents are occasionally transferred from the nursing home to the hospital for certain medical conditions that cannot be treated at the nursing home. Upon the resident's return to the nursing home, a new medical record is often started and the old chart is put in some sort of document storage.

Unfortunately, the new medical record does not assist emergency personnel should your parent need to be transferred to the hospital. The new records do not contain the bulk of his past history and treatment. If you have copies of these records, you can provide them to an outside doctor who treats your parent in the event the nursing home either begins a new chart or misplaces his records.

The second reason for periodically acquiring copies of your parent's medical records is because some nursing homes have been known to refuse to provide these records to legal representatives. If your relationship with the facility should ever sour, which is not a rare occurrence, you already have a head start in the documentation collection process. I am not suggesting that you immediately prepare yourself for a potential legal battle by hoarding these records, but I do want to be clear that you are entitled to these records and there are plenty of facilities that have refused to honor a request for records despite this entitlement.

I recommend getting copies of your parent's current medical chart once a year and after every hospital transfer and/or significant medical event. Facilities have also been known to "thin" medical records that become too thick after months or years of treatment by placing older documents in storage.

LEGAL REPRESENTATIVES

Your parent should have one of the following types of representation in effect while in the nursing home:

POA (power of attorney): A document created by a mentally competent individual to appoint another person to handle his or her affairs.

DPOA (durable power of attorney): A document created by a mentally competent individual to appoint another person to handle his or her affairs. This document retains its agency power even if/when the mentally competent individual who issued the authority becomes incompetent.

MPOA (medical power of attorney): A document created by a mentally competent individual to appoint another person to make health care decisions on his or her behalf in the event that the mentally competent person becomes incapable of making those decisions for himself or herself.

Guardian: An individual appointed by the court to act on behalf of a resident who is incapable of managing his or her financial and/or medical affairs. The guardian can be a lawyer, a nurse, a social worker, a family member, or a friend. Talk to the facility social worker and/or an eldercare attorney to determine which type of representation your parent should have.

§483.10(a)(3). *In the case of a resident adjudged incompetent under the laws of a State by a court of competent jurisdiction, the rights of the resident are exercised by the person appointed under State law to act on the resident's behalf.*

This regulation allows a guardian to act on behalf of a resident who has been declared incompetent in order to assert any right that is afforded the resident. In such a case, the guardian appointed to act on the resident's behalf is entitled to seek enforcement of all rights to which the resident is entitled.

§483.10(a)(4). *In the case of a resident who has not been adjudged incompetent by the State court, any legal surrogate designated in accordance with State law may exercise the resident's rights to the extent provided by State law.*

This regulation allows a resident to have others act on his or her behalf. A competent resident may empower a delegate to enforce rights on his or her behalf. However, the facility must secure health care decisions from the resident and not from a legal representative if the resident is competent to make those decisions.

§483.10(b)(4). *The resident has the right to refuse treatment, to refuse to participate in experimental research, and to formulate an advance directive.*

This regulation encompasses three entitlements. The first part stipulates that your parent can refuse any form of treatment, even if it is a treatment that is necessary for survival. Your parent has the right to exercise his or her own judgment and the right to make decisions that may be contrary to traditional medical advice.

I believe nursing home staff has the most difficulty with this regulation when it comes to allowing residents to refuse meals and medications. Food and medication are often seen as the fuel that keeps residents alive and strong. While it may be true that the staff knows what is best for the longevity of the resident, the resident still has the option of choosing which treatments he or she will accept.

What I have observed over the years is that the nursing home staff wants the residents to accept their medication and meals. Some staff members can be overly aggressive in their attempts to get residents to comply with meal plans and medication orders. I have seen many residents try to turn their heads away from their meals, only to have a staff member place a hand on their head and physically turn them back toward the spoon. At more than one facility I have witnessed a nursing assistant pinch shut a resident's nose to force her to open her mouth. This type of power struggle does not occur often, since most nursing assistants are pressed for time and usually will stop trying to feed the resident at the first sign of disinterest.

Nurses also want residents to accept their medications in order to promote comfort and longevity. Also, if a patient has disruptive nervous tendencies, medication with a calming or sedative effect might be desirable. Many times, residents turn their heads away from the medication or flat out say, "No, I don't want it." But some nurses can be insistent. "C'mon, take your medicine, it will help such and such" or "If you take your medication, I'll take you to the television room." This back-and-forth dialogue can go on for several minutes until either the nurse accepts that the resident has refused or the resident succumbs to the repeated requests.

Residents also have the right to refuse experimental treatments. If you are your parent's legal representative, you have the power to refuse on his or her behalf.

The third part of this regulation allows your parent to create advance medical directives, which provide specific written instructions to caregivers in advance of an injury or illness. Advance directives allow your parent to indicate which procedures she wants performed in order to save or prolong her life. The directives generally cover the decision to insert or refuse a feeding tube in the event she is no longer able to ingest food by mouth, whether she wants to be resuscitated in the event of respiratory or cardiac failure, and whether she would want to be connected to a mechanical ventilator or breathing machine.

You Should Know that the information in the advance directive documents is not always readily accessible by the nursing staff in an emergency situation. If the nurse is new to the unit, he may be unfamiliar with the filing system and therefore may not be able to quickly locate these important documents. Sometimes, the documents get lost or misplaced.

A sudden medical emergency may arise in which the staff doesn't know which procedures the resident does or does not want. In such a case, the hunt for the medical documentation is usually an after-thought. For instance, if a nurse does not know whether a particular resident has refused cardiopulmonary resuscitation, and that resident is in immediate need of such a procedure, she will usually administer CPR rather than search for the previously documented instructions. However, sometimes the reverse is true, and residents are denied emergency care based on the nurse's assumption that the resident did not want resuscitative efforts performed.

Another unfortunate scenario occurs when a resident is rushed to the hospital without the advance directive documentation. The emergency room physician has no way of knowing the resident's previously documented wishes and so must err on the side of caution. To avoid such a situation, submit copies of the documents to the hospital your parent would most likely be transferred to. Since most nursing homes are usually affiliated with and transfer all their residents to the same hospital, you should be able to communicate your parent's wishes beforehand rather than rely on the nursing home staff to provide the information to the hospital.

RIGHT TO PRIVACY

§483.15 (e) (2). *The resident has the right to receive notice before the resident's room or roommate in the facility is changed.*

Residents frequently have their room or roommate changed due to a request, the discharge or death of a resident, or a change in a resident's condition that requires a transfer to a specialty unit. I have repeatedly seen the same residents moved over and over to accommodate the needs of other residents. Usually, the residents who are moved are the ones who are unable to object to the room change.

You Should Know that room changes occur often and are a major inconvenience to the resident. Quite often a resident learns of the room change as the furniture is being moved, and not one minute sooner. If your parent did not initiate the move, tell the facility you do not want your parent moved unless it is absolutely necessary.

It is certainly an adjustment to get a new roommate, but it is much more difficult to be the resident who is frequently moved. I have seen residents consent to room changes they did not want, but they preferred not to take a stand against the issue. Most residents, even when asked, do not assert themselves enough to object to a move. They would rather maintain a peaceful existence and not appear argumentative.

After moving to a new room, many residents become confused about its location. Once a resident establishes and maintains a routine, it can be difficult or even traumatic to be uprooted from all that is familiar and have to adjust to a new environment. Residents with a firm-handed family member will never be considered a candidate for a room change if that move is motivated by convenience of the facility. Instead, the facility will know that you are a strong advocate for your parent and that you will provide steadfast opposition if your parent is moved unnecessarily.

At one facility, I saw several mentally alert and able residents moved from the long-term-care unit to the Alzheimer's unit to make room for additional long-term-care residents. These residents were completely oriented and aware of their surroundings. They certainly did not belong on an Alzheimer's unit. Because they "agreed" to the move and had no family members who objected to the transfer, these active, vibrant residents lived miserably on a locked unit among Alzheimer's residents until enough nurses expressed their complaints about the arrangement. After the nurses firmly requested that the facility not put mentally cognizant residents on the Alzheimer's unit, the facility managers moved the residents back to the long-term-care unit.

§483.10(i)(2). *The resident has the right to have access to stationery, postage, and writing implements at the resident's own expense.*

The resident has a right to purchase and possess his own stationery, stamps, and pens/pencils.

§483.15(c)(1). *A resident has the right to organize and participate in resident groups in the facility.*

Residents who are interested in forming a group to discuss issues regarding the facility have a right to do so without interference from the facility management. If such a group already exists, your parent has the right to join the group. If such a group does not exist, your parent has the right to initiate the group's formation. The facility must provide a private place for the group to meet and a staff person to act as an intermediary between the group and the facility.

This type of group is usually called a Resident Council. The members get together to discuss and brainstorm any issues regarding the operation of the nursing home and to determine which areas need improvement. Popular topics at such meetings are the quality of food, understaffing, and types of activities.

You Should Know that the topics of discussion at these meetings are often summarized in writing and maintained at the facility. You should review these minutes to determine the main concerns among the nursing home population. Your parent, if able, should be attending these meetings in order to voice his or her opinions and help the group discover and resolve issues.

§483.15(c)(2). *A resident's family has the right to meet in the facility with the families of other residents in the facility.*

Like the residents' group, the family group discusses issues regarding the facility and the delivery of care. This group is usually called a Family Council. The facility must provide a private place for the group to meet and a staff member to act as an intermediary between the group and the facility.

You Should Know that residents whose families actively participate in their care receive more attentive treatment than those residents with passive or absent family members. If you are a family member, you should join the council to learn more about the facility and to offer your own opinions and comments. If your facility does not have a Family Council, you should establish one or attend the Resident Council meetings. You can review the minutes of these meetings by asking the administrator for a copy.

RIGHT TO BE FREE FROM RESTRAINTS AND ABUSE

§483.13(a). *The resident has the right to be free from any physical or chemical restraints imposed for purposes of discipline or convenience and not required to treat the resident's medical symptoms.*

The nursing home staff cannot tie residents to a chair or bed simply because they do not have enough staff to properly care for all of the residents, nor can the staff use medication as a restraint in order to lessen its responsibility to monitor and care for the residents.

These types of physical restraints can be belts, vests, or ties that restrict a resident's movement. Such devices were used openly and frequently in years past, but their use has significantly decreased since the enactment of the Nursing Home Reform Act; however, their use has not been entirely abolished.

Chemical restraints are medications that are used to calm, quiet, or subdue a resident, thereby eliminating the possibility of mobility. With these medications, a resident's movement is restricted to the point where he or she is unable to stand or move independently. This type of medication might be scheduled regularly around the clock or administered only as the staff deems necessary.

You Should Know that both physical and chemical restraints are still used at many facilities. I have seen wheelchairs locked and pushed against a table or desk to keep residents from standing or moving away from a designated area. I have seen staff members prop up the footrest of a recliner chair using a small table in order to prevent the resident from lowering the footrest and getting out of the chair.

Very often, nursing assistants will sit next to residents while they do their paperwork and hold the back of a resident's shirt, pulling him back into the chair if he attempts to stand. Or, staff members simply tell the residents to "sit down" each time they attempt to stand, even when the resident repeatedly says, "I have to go to the bathroom." I have heard a few nursing assistants yell, "I am not going to tell you again, sit down!"

The nursing assistants are put in the impossible situation of being required to complete their paperwork thoroughly and accurately, yet they are never relieved of their direct-care responsibilities. They either rush and fudge the paperwork or temporarily restrain the residents who require constant supervision—or both—in order to meet the demands of their multifaceted jobs.

The most common type of restraint that I have seen used is sedative medication. Many nursing home residents with behavioral issues have an arsenal of medications available to be given on an as-needed basis. Because the medication order is usually to be given as directed "for agitation, anxiety, or nervousness," the nurse on duty is allowed to use her subjective judgment to determine if a resident needs to be medicated.

For instance, many residents have physician orders to receive medications on an as-needed basis, which grants the nurse a great deal of power. The day shift nurse could give your parent Tylenol for the same pain that a nurse on the evening shift might administer Percocet, provided your parent has a physician's order for both medications.

Some nurses reach for the antianxiety medication at the first sign of feistiness, while others try a different approach, perhaps using soft music, a tempting snack, going for a walk, or some other activity to help a resident calm down. Some residents have a multitude of medication available to them for a variety of conditions. I have seen numerous nurses give a narcotic pain medication along with an antianxiety medication to be certain that a resident will be sufficiently subdued. If a resident who is known to be boisterous becomes even slightly agitated, the nurse will administer anything and everything to prevent disruptive behavior that he does not have the staff to handle.

Many times residents are medicated for anxiety when the cause of the anxiety is created by poor staffing. A resident may exhibit signs of frustration over the fact that no one has answered her call bell in thirty minutes. The resident's angry reaction is often interpreted as anxiety. The fact that the resident cannot adequately articulate her needs may also be interpreted as anxiety.

I have seen residents medicated because another resident has angered them. I have seen residents medicated preventively simply because they woke up and were likely to become bothersome to staff. Most disturbingly, I have seen residents receive antianxiety medication on a scheduled, routine basis, and kept in a semi-sedated state at all times. In a busy, understaffed nursing home, medication is the easiest and most reliable way to keep residents under control.

§483.13(b). *The resident has the right to be free from verbal, sexual, physical, and mental abuse, corporal punishment, and involuntary seclusion.*

Residents have a right to be free from abuse from nursing home staff, family members, visitors, other residents, and any other person residents come into contact with during their stay. The nursing home is responsible for the safety and well-being of its residents at all times.

You Should Know that this regulation is frequently violated. Degrading comments such as "You just went to the bathroom an hour ago." "Didn't I just take you to the bathroom?" "What are you ringing for now? I was just in here." And "Your clothes are wet again, (sigh) c'mon, let's go back to your room and change your clothes all over again" are directed toward nursing home residents every day.

Even more alarming is the fact that sexual abuse against residents occurs in nursing homes regularly. Nursing home employees are frequently arrested and charged with sexually abusing elderly residents (see chapter 7). The screening process of prospective employees is designed to prevent sexual predators from working in nursing homes, but it is not always an effective means of keeping residents safe.

I once worked at a nursing home where a female resident was visited by her husband nearly every day. While the husband visited his wife, who had Alzheimer's disease, he repeatedly sexually abused his wife's roommate. Once the abuse was discovered, future visits with his wife had to be monitored by nursing home staff. To my knowledge, no criminal charges were ever filed against the abuser.

Derogatory comments that intimidate or humiliate residents are a form of mental abuse. Comments such as "I can't put you onto your bed by myself because you're too heavy; I need to find someone to help me. I'm not going to hurt my back by doing it myself" constitute verbal and mental abuse of the resident, especially when made in front of other people.

On the occasions that I witnessed and reported verbally abusive behavior, I discovered that the facility was not interested in investigating complaints unless there was an actual physical altercation or obvious injury. I know of one nurse who reported a nursing assistant for abusive behavior and, instead of having the event investigated, he was accused of fabricating the event.

Now that you are acquainted with many of the entitlements of nursing home residents and the persistent problems that plague most nursing homes, you probably see the need for a more specific version of the Residents' Rights.

The regulations that govern nursing homes grant every nursing home resident the right to a dignified existence, yet residents continue to suffer the same indignities that the laws prohibit. With all statutory pleasantries and ambiguities aside, I have prepared a more precise version of the rights that nursing homes should honor.

I've seen each of these "rights" violated with such regularity that they *should* be specifically written and obeyed, rather than implied in the regulation. Every resident should be able to assert the right

- to be taken off a bedpan before a bright red indentation forms on his or her backside
- to be helped off of the toilet before he gets so uncomfortable that he tries to get up alone and falls as a result
- to be cleaned of excrement before feeling ashamed, embarrassed, or developing skin irritation
- to be relieved of constipation before having to be rushed to the hospital with severe abdominal pain
- to be spoken to like an adult, not like a child, when requesting help to the bathroom
- to be spoken to in a respectful manner and never snapped at
- to be included in conversations that concern him or her
- to not have staff members talk about him or her while in his or her presence
- to have the call bell answered promptly and not be avoided for being heavier, weaker, or more difficult than other residents
- to be asked if he or she would like to do something, not have staff announce that it is time for something
- to be taken care of at an appropriate pace and not feel rushed during care
- to be cared for by staff members who show a genuine concern for the well-being of others and not an obvious disdain for their profession
- to be cared for by staff members who are not sick with a cold, sore throat, or other infectious illness

CHAPTER 4

LEGAL REQUIREMENTS OF THE NURSING HOME

*"I've had my call bell on for twenty minutes. It's too late,
I've already wet the sheets. I'm sorry."*
—nursing home resident after nursing home resident after nursing home
resident after nursing home resident

The Nursing Home Reform Act requires nursing homes to assume the responsibility of meeting the individual needs of each resident. This chapter introduces additional regulations that I believe are frequently violated or are likely to be violated. These regulations dictate the specific actions the facility must take to ensure proper care is delivered to each resident.

These regulations are not mere recommendations that the facilities may *choose* to obey; they are laws that the facilities are *required* to follow. When nursing homes fail to comply with the act, they are breaking the law.

THE FACILITY MUST INFORM THE RESIDENT/FAMILY

§483.10(b)(9). *The facility must inform each resident of the name, specialty, and way of contacting the physician responsible for his or her care.*

This regulation requires the facility to give the resident a method by which he or she can contact the doctor. Such communication between resident and doctor almost always occurs through the nurse on duty. The nurse acts as an intermediary between the two, deciding whether the doctor should be called, especially after hours or on weekends.

Nurses are advised to use their own judgment regarding when to contact the doctor on behalf of a resident. For instance, if a resident wants to see the doctor for a headache, the nurse can consult the "standing orders," which are orders the doctor has written in anticipation of a resident having a headache. Standing orders usually encompass medication orders for conditions such as nausea, diarrhea, cold symptoms, indigestion, or constipation. A common standing order may read "For constipation give Milk of Magnesia 30 ml by mouth once per day." The doctor usually lists ten or fifteen medications the nurse can administer without contacting the doctor.

Most nurses will give residents a medication from the list, if possible, to avoid calling the doctor. Other nurses call the doctor each time a resident requests that the nurse do so, even if that means calling every thirty minutes. It is completely discretionary. Rarely does the facility give the doctor's telephone number to the resident or the resident's family. However, you should ask for it anyway, and if you get it, write it down in the appropriate chart in chapter 8.

§483.10(b)(11)(i)(A). *The facility must immediately inform the resident; consult with the resident's physician; and if known, notify the resident's legal representative or an interested family member when there is an accident involving the resident which results in injury and has the potential for requiring physician intervention.*

This regulation requires the facility to immediately contact the doctor and the resident's family member or representative when a resident has an accident or injury that may require the doctor to intervene. If a competent resident invokes his or her right to privacy, the facility does not need to notify the family.

All the facilities where I have either worked or visited use a form called an "Incident Report." An Incident Report is filled out by the nurse on duty after an incident or accident involving a resident. Its most common use is for a resident who falls, but it is also used when a resident is struck by another resident, obtains a bruise or skin tear during direct care from a staff member, or is otherwise injured. The form includes a check-the-box section that serves as a reminder to the nurse to contact the family and the doctor.

If the injury occurs late at night, which happens often, the night nurse will usually leave instructions for the next shift to notify the family to avoid having to make a call in the middle of the night. Unfortunately, in a facility with a poor communication system between shifts, calling the family after an accident is often overlooked. I cannot tell you how many times I have heard family members complain that they were never notified of an accident involving their parent.

Other forms may accompany the Incident Report, such as witness statements and flow sheets, which are a chronological record of vital signs or neurological assessments performed immediately after the incident. If the incident resulted in a head injury, such assessments are typically performed every fifteen or thirty minutes for at least a few hours after the accident. These forms should be part of your parent's medical record, although sometimes they are not.

You Should Know that if your parent is injured at the nursing home, you are entitled to have access to the Incident Report and the accompanying forms. The information in an Incident Report includes the type of injury sustained, how the incident happened, what could have been done to prevent the incident, and the names of witnesses.

I worked in one facility that had the following statement printed in bold letters across the top of the incident report: **"This form is being completed in anticipation of litigation: the contents herein are considered confidential."** The reason this particular facility chose to print that statement at the top of its Incident Reports was to attempt to avoid disclosing the information in the form. Regardless of whether or not you are permitted access to the form, you should get the following four pieces of information from the director of nurses after an accident.

First, you want to know the nature of the accident. Was your parent hit by another resident? Did he or she fall out of bed? You want to know exactly what happened. Second, what is the facility doing to ensure that this incident does not recur? Having all possible information about prevention measures will help you communicate with the managers in the event that your parent continues to fall out of bed or to be struck by another resident. It will be easier for you to ask the director of nurses to account for the reasons why the incident keeps happening if you have already determined what was supposed to have been done to prevent the repeated injury.

Third, you want to know what type of injury your parent sustained and whether the doctor was notified. If the doctor was not notified, insist that he or she be notified and that your parent be physically evaluated by the doctor. If the injury is serious, you should also report the incident to the state agency that inspects your parent's facility.

Beware. I have heard plenty of nurses ask a resident, "You don't want me to call your family, do you?" or "We don't need to worry your son about this, right?" I have even heard this type of question asked of residents who are confused and not able to make their own medical decisions. The nurse is usually so bogged down with the incident, the resident's injury, and the ensuing paperwork that any step eliminated is time saved.

Finally, retain as much documented information about the incident as possible. You want to be able to present this information to a hospital physician in an organized fashion, if necessary. There is an injury chart located in chapter 8 that will help you categorize the information. You will not need to go through these steps if the incident was minor in nature.

§483.10(b)(11)(i)(B). *The facility must immediately inform the resident; consult with the resident's physician; and if known, notify the resident's legal representative or an interested family member when there is a significant change in the resident's physical, mental, or psychosocial status (i.e., a deterioration in health, mental, or psychosocial status in either life-threatening conditions or clinical complications).*

This regulation requires the facility to immediately contact the doctor and the resident's family member or representative when a resident's condition changes significantly. A significant change would include stroke, serious injury or infection, behavioral changes, or any kind of life-threatening medical event. If a competent resident invokes his or her right to privacy, however, the facility does not need to notify the family.

§483.10(b)(11)(i)(C). *The facility must immediately inform the resident; consult with the resident's physician; and if known, notify the resident's legal representative or an interested family member when there is a need to alter treatment significantly (i.e., a need to discontinue an existing form of treatment due to adverse consequences, or to commence a new form of treatment).*

This regulation requires the facility to immediately contact the doctor and the resident's family member or representative when a resident's treatment plan is changed significantly.

Many facilities automatically notify the family when there is a change in a resident's medications, while others do not. Some facilities require the family to sign a permission form indicating consent to the use of the medication, usually for behavior-altering drugs. The facility should notify you any time a medication is stopped, started, or changed. You should let the director of nurses know that you want to be notified of *all* medication changes, regardless of their significance.

You Should Know what medications your parent is taking. Some medications require frequent blood level monitoring to ensure that the proper amount of medication is in the bloodstream at all times. The blood thinner Coumadin is one such medication and is given in conjunction with monthly blood draws. I have seen this medication given to numerous residents whose physician orders for monthly blood draws were not followed due to faulty procedures. There was no system in place to alert the nurses that a blood draw was due each month.

I was on duty one evening when a resident who began to bleed profusely from an injury to her mouth was found to have skipped her monthly blood draw for six consecutive months. She was transferred to the hospital to treat the uncontrollable bleeding. Had it not been for her injury, she would have continued to receive her Coumadin.

Many medications cause side effects that range from subtle and harmless to outright dangerous. You cannot consistently rely on the nursing home staff to immediately detect changes in your parent's behavior if the facility is understaffed, if the staff comes mainly from a nursing agency, or if the staff is otherwise unfamiliar with your parent.

Every medication will not affect every person the same way. Some medications, like narcotics, commonly cause constipation in the elderly and call for close scrutiny of a resident's bowel pattern. Quite often residents are placed on a narcotic medication for pain management, and their inability to have a bowel movement goes undetected for several days. I have seen numerous residents on a new pain medication go eight or nine days without a documented bowel movement.

I have also seen some residents who received laxatives every few days while also getting an antidiarrhea medication. I know of one resident who received eight doses of laxatives in a one-month period for her constipation. She also received eight doses of antidiarrhea medication between the days of constipation. That means that approximately every other day she received either an antidiarrhea medication or a laxative. The doctor did not even know that this seesaw game between medications had occurred, since both of these medications were on the list of standing orders. When you review your parent's medical record, you will see which medications your parent received, including those from the standing order list.

Finally, some medications are ordered for only a certain number of days or weeks but are not stopped on the intended date. If you know when and why a medication is started, you may be able to prevent a medication error from occurring.

When the nursing home physician places your parent on a new medication, you should learn about the intended benefits, the potential side effects, the length of time for which it is ordered, and whether your parent requires a regular blood level check.

§483.10(b)(11)(ii)(A). *The facility must also promptly notify the resident, and if known, the resident's legal representative or interested family member when there is a change in room or roommate assignment as specified in §483.15(e)(2).*

This regulation prevents the facility from making room changes without prior notification. You should never have to learn of a room or roommate change after it has already taken place. You should always be notified in advance of the change and be given the opportunity to discuss it, if necessary.

§483.10(b)(11)(iii). *The facility must record and periodically update the address and phone number of the resident's legal representative or interested family member.*

This regulation requires the facility to maintain current contact information for the interested family member of the resident. In reality, the burden is on the family to provide new information to the facility each time there is an address or telephone number change.

At most facilities, the family contact information for each resident is conveniently located on the first page of the medical chart. You should review it for accuracy.

THE FACILITY MUST POST INFORMATION

§483.10(b)(7)(iii). *The facility must furnish a written description of legal rights which includes a posting of names, addresses, and telephone numbers of all pertinent State client advocacy groups such as the State survey and certification agency, the State licensure office, the State ombudsman program, the protection and advocacy network, and the Medicaid fraud control unit.*

§483.10(b)(7)(iv). *The facility must furnish a written description of legal rights which includes a statement that the resident may file a complaint with the State survey and certification agency concerning resident abuse, neglect,* *misappropriation of resident property in the facility, and noncompliance with the advance directives requirements.*

Both of these regulations require facilities to provide these names, numbers, and addresses to each resident. The nursing home should post this information at the entrance to the facility and/or provide it in the admission paperwork. All of these telephone numbers should be entered in the appropriate chart in chapter 8.

§483.10(j)(3). *The facility must allow representatives of the State Ombudsman, described in paragraph (j)(l)(iv) of this section, to examine a resident's clinical records with the permission of the resident or the resident's legal representative, and consistent with State law.*

This regulation requires the facility to allow investigators from the ombudsman's office access to the resident's medical record. Such access is necessary to the complaint process. Once a resident, or a person acting on behalf of a resident, files a complaint with the ombudsman's office, the investigators review the medical chart. The investigation may also include interviewing witnesses.

§483.30(e)(1)(iii). *The facility must post the following information on a daily basis: the total number and the actual hours worked by the following categories of licensed and unlicensed nursing staff directly responsible for resident care per shift: registered nurses, licensed practical nurses or licensed vocational nurses, certified nurse aides.*

Each day, the names, titles, and shifts of the nursing employees on duty should be posted in a location convenient to residents and their families. The facility is required to post the staffing information as well as the current resident census. Look for names that have been circled, crossed off the list, or otherwise marked. Such markings usually indicate who will not be coming in to work, so checking this list will keep you from being misled into thinking there are more people on duty. Sick calls are common in the nursing home business, and the posted list may not be updated throughout the day as schedule changes occur.

§483.30(e)(2)(ii). *The facility must post the nurse staffing data (A) in a clear and readable format and (B) in a prominent place readily accessible to residents and visitors.*

Although this information indicates the ratio for the entire facility, it does not specifically indicate the ratio on the unit where your parent resides. Before you check this posting, be sure you have asked the director of nurses what the staffing should be each day so that you will know how frequently the facility falls below its staffing policies. I worked in a facility with forty-five residents on a particular unit. Both long-term-care and skilled-care residents lived on the unit. The facility instituted a policy whereby no fewer than five nursing assistants were ever scheduled to work the day shift, yet the unit consistently operated with only four nursing assistants.

§483.30(e)(3). *The facility must, upon oral or written request, make nurse staffing data available to the public for review at a cost not to exceed the community standard.*

Staffing information is available to you even if you do not currently have a family member living in the facility. If your parent has not yet moved into a nursing home and you are looking at prospective nursing homes for the first time, you are able to review staffing information beforehand. This information is also valuable to those who want to compare their current facility to other area facilities.

§483.30(e)(4). *The facility must maintain the posted daily nurse staffing data for a minimum of 18 months, or as required by State law, whichever is greater.*

Since the facility must keep staffing data for eighteen months, you should be able to calculate a rough average staff-to-resident ratio.

THE FACILITY MUST ASSESS THE NEEDS OF THE RESIDENT

§483.20. *The facility must conduct initially and periodically a comprehensive, accurate, standardized, reproducible assessment of each resident's functional capacity.*

This regulation requires the facility to accurately assess each resident's needs and abilities at the time he or she is admitted to the nursing home and at periodic intervals during his or her stay in order to determine and plan what type of care to deliver.

The initial assessment of a resident admitted to a nursing home includes a complete assessment of the resident's skin, mental status and ability, physical mobility, fall risk, nutritional status, and medications. This admission assessment is done primarily by the nurse on duty at the time of the admission.

I have worked in a few nursing homes that schedule an additional nurse specifically for the purpose of handling the incoming resident(s) since it is a very time-consuming process to perform a complete physical and mental assessment. However, I have also worked in several facilities that do not provide additional nursing staff when a resident is admitted, and therefore the admission process is rushed because the nurse has no extra time to complete an assessment and admission paperwork in addition to her scheduled duties. In such cases, the staff may not learn all pertinent information about your parent immediately upon admission.

Some facilities break up the responsibilities over several shifts so the entire assessment need not be rushed by one nurse. The first nurse may conduct the fall assessment while the second nurse may do the skin check, and so on. I will tell you that if your parent's initial admission assessment is done by a nurse who is also caring for an entire unit, some information about your parent will likely fall through the cracks. If possible, you should be present for the admission process to alert staff about important care issues.

The immediate goal for the nurse who makes initial contact with the resident upon his or her admission is to determine what medications the resident is taking and to order them from the pharmacy. Medication administration is a major issue for every nursing home because most residents take a multitude of pills and most nursing hours are devoted to distributing these pills. I have heard many residents complain that they "never took so many medications until coming into the nursing home."

Of course, there are other steps of the admission process that should be completed as soon as the new resident arrives, such as orienting him to his room, determining whether a fall risk exists, planning to meet dietary needs, assessing the resident's mental status and any potential safety hazards, and starting a medical record.

As with all other duties, there are time constraints on performing an initial admission assessment as well as the periodic assessments. Nurses must conduct the periodic assessment, usually done every three months, very quickly and they often do not even know the residents they are assessing.

Many nursing homes divide these quarterly assessment responsibilities among the staff nurses. I once received a list of eight residents who needed assessments. I had seldom worked on the unit where those residents lived, so I hardly knew them. I was on an understaffed evening shift and did not have time to do the assessments until the residents were already in bed. I found myself asking the nursing assistants, "Does she use the bathroom on her own, or is she incontinent?" "Does he feed himself or does he need to be fed?"

Many times, information that is already of record is simply rerecorded from the prior assessment to the current assessment because many nurses are not familiar with the abilities of the residents and do not have the time to personally and accurately determine them. The nurses' rationale for rerecording existing information is that a resident who is suddenly awakened cannot reliably display his or her mental and physical status. In my opinion, these assessments should be done only by nurses who regularly work and have familiarity with the residents. Nevertheless, I know of a few facilities that require agency and per diem nurses to complete the quarterly assessments.

§483.20(a). *At the time each resident is admitted, the facility must have physician orders for the resident's immediate care.*

Nursing home staff is not permitted to provide care to a resident without a physician's order to do so. The doctor is typically notified that the resident has arrived at the nursing home, and she either writes treatment orders in person or dictates them to the nurse over the telephone.

§483.20(d). *The facility must maintain all resident assessments completed within the previous 15 months in the resident's active record and use the results of the assessments to develop, review, and revise the resident's comprehensive plan of care.*

This regulation requires the facility to keep the assessments in the medical chart for fifteen months and to use them for the creation of the plan of care. When you obtain copies of your parent's medical records, you will be able to review the assessments. If the records you receive do not include the assessments, be sure to insist on getting copies of those records as well. You should review these assessments for accuracy.

§483.20(k)(1). *The facility must develop a comprehensive care plan for each resident that includes measurable objectives and timetables to meet a resident's medical, nursing, and mental and psychosocial needs that are identified in the comprehensive assessment.*

This regulation requires the facility to create a care plan for each resident. The care plan should describe the resident's goals and the steps necessary to meet those goals. Every time a resident needs a particular service, the care plan should describe how that service will be delivered. The length of time required by the resident to meet those goals should also be documented in the care plan. The care plan is kept in the resident's medical chart and should be continually updated to reflect the changing needs of the resident.

It is my assertion that these care plans are rarely looked at by the nurses who deliver your parent's care. In fact, the resident's medical chart is not routinely checked by the nurse on duty. This is because the nurse on duty spends the majority of his eight-hour shift passing out medications and refers mainly to the medication book, which lists all residents by name and which medications they are to receive. The medical chart, which is separate from the medication book, contains all pertinent information regarding your parent, including recent nurse notes, assessments, and the care plan. Certainly, the nurse consults your parent's medical chart when an incident occurs, but you should not be under the misguided impression that your parent's care plan is reviewed regularly by every nurse. Even if every care plan was removed from each medical chart and handed to the nurse at the beginning of his shift, he would not have time to review each one. Only the nurses who work regularly on your parent's unit will be familiar with the information in his or her medical chart.

You Should Know what is included in your parent's care plan. If you are familiar with the plan of care, you will easily detect any deviation and more readily recognize a treatment that may be inconsistent with that plan. Knowing the details of your parent's care plan will also enable you to better assist your parent in reaching his or her goals.

§483.20(k)(1)(i). *The care plan must describe the services that are to be furnished to attain or maintain the resident's highest practicable physical, mental, and psychosocial well-being.*

The care plan must outline what services the facility plans to provide and what actions the staff plans to take during the course of caring for your parent to ensure his or her well-being. The sooner you become aware of these proposed services and treatments, the sooner you will notice whether or not they are being delivered.

§483.25. *Each resident must receive and the facility must provide the necessary care and services to attain or maintain the highest practicable physical, mental, and psychosocial well-being, in accordance with the comprehensive assessment and plan of care.*

The facility must deliver—not merely devise a plan to deliver—the services each resident requires in order to thrive. The services must promote each resident's ability to live a quality life to his or her full potential.

§483.40(c)(1). *The resident must be seen by a physician at least once every 30 days for the first 90 days after admission, and at least once every 60 days thereafter.*

A nurse practitioner or a physician's assistant is permitted to see the resident in place of the physician in order to meet this requirement.

THE FACILITY MUST PROVIDE ADEQUATE CARE

§483.25(a)(1). *The facility must ensure that a resident's abilities in activities of daily living do not diminish unless circumstances of the individual's clinical condition demonstrate that diminution is unavoidable.*

Your parent's ability to bathe, walk, go to the restroom, and eat should not decrease unless the deterioration in those capabilities is unavoidable. The nursing home staff must put forth the necessary effort for your parent to maintain or improve his current level of functioning. If a resident has the ability to walk, albeit with assistance, he should not lose that ability simply because the facility does not have the available staff to walk with him.

§483.25(a)(3). *The facility must ensure that a resident who is unable to carry out activities of daily living receives necessary services to maintain good nutrition, grooming, and personal and oral hygiene.*

Your parent, if unable to eat and bathe independently, shall be fed and bathed by the nursing home staff. The facility should allow the staff members sufficient time to carry out each task.

§483.25(b)(1–2). *The facility must, if necessary, assist the resident in (1) making appointments, and (2) by arranging for transportation to and from the office of a practitioner specializing in the treatment of vision or hearing impairment or the office of a professional specializing in the provision of vision or hearing assistive devices.*

The nursing home staff should assist your parent in obtaining vision and hearing examinations, corrective eyewear, and hearing aids. The facility should help your parent make the appointments and provide transportation.

§483.55(a)(4). *The facility must promptly refer residents with lost or damaged dentures to a dentist.*

If your parent has dentures that do not fit properly, the facility must acknowledge the problem and make arrangements for remedial care. Many residents simply do not wear their dentures because they find them too uncomfortable. Rather than replace or repair ill-fitting dentures, a facility might change a resident's diet to soft foods.

I have seen residents go for several months without their dentures because no one bothered to look for the lost dentures or go about replacing them. If lost dentures are not located within a reasonable length of time, they need to be replaced.

§483.25(c)(1). *The facility must ensure that a resident who enters the facility without pressure sores does not develop pressure sores unless the individual's clinical condition demonstrates that they were unavoidable.*

Your parent should be assessed for susceptibility to pressure sores upon entry to the nursing home. If found to be at risk for pressure sores, the nursing home staff must take the necessary steps to ensure that your parent receives treatment in accordance with the facility's prevention protocol. The facility must ensure that your parent does not remain in the same position for an extended period of time and that he receives adequate nutrition and skin care to prevent skin breakdown.

§483.25(c)(2). *The facility must ensure that a resident having pressure sores receives necessary treatment and services to promote healing, prevent infection, and prevent new sores from developing.*

If your parent is admitted to the nursing home with a pressure sore or if he develops one after admission, the nursing home staff must take the necessary steps to heal it and prevent new sores from developing. The staff must keep it clean and free of infection. This usually includes keeping the wound bandaged, or dressed. But as you know by now, not all treatment orders are strictly followed.

I once finished up my shift just as another nurse was leaving. We agreed that the shift was too short to get everything done that was required of us. She said, "Nobody can do all of the treatments." She added nonchalantly, "Everyone signs them off without actually doing them."

It was not what she said that surprised me; I had known for years that many treatments were being signed off without actually being done. However, I was struck by the way she seemed to accept this practice, as if it were okay to make it look as though as we had enough staff to do the job right. My concern was that the facility managers would never change the staffing situation if nurses were signing their names to work they had no time to complete, making it seem like there was no problem with staffing.

Based on what I have seen in nursing homes, I am willing to bet that every nurse knows another nurse who frequently skips most of the scheduled treatments. I have heard nurses at nearly every nursing home talk about another nurse's practices: "There is no way she had time to do all of her treatments" or "I know she hasn't done any treatments in three days."

As I indicated in chapter 2, I, too, have faced the reality that I could not get it all done. The result is a feeling of inadequacy after having "lost the race." Admittedly, I have taken shortcuts and prioritized my treatments. For example, if one resident needed a closed-wound treatment and another needed a dressing changed on a gaping wound, the open-wound treatment was top priority. Closed-wound treatments are sometimes skipped if the nurse's time is limited.

Treatments such as foot soaks, scalp conditioning, rash creams, and oral rinses are considered low priority, particularly if there is an urgent need for attention, such as an open wound. The name of the game in nursing home care is prioritization, especially when the staffing is extremely low. Missing an occasional closed-wound treatment is not necessarily a problem, but the reality is that at some time or another, every nurse makes an occasional treatment omission. Continued treatment omissions could deprive your parent not only of the treatment but of the chance for a visual inspection of the wound, which, consequently, is likely to worsen.

§483.25(d)(1). *The facility must ensure that a resident who enters the facility without an indwelling catheter is not catheterized unless the resident's clinical condition demonstrates that catheterization was necessary.*

The primary purpose of such a catheter is to allow for the drainage of urine when the resident is unable to voluntarily urinate. This regulation forbids the facility from inserting a catheter unless it is absolutely necessary. Catheters should not be used for the convenience of the staff just because a resident is frequently incontinent. These catheters also require a doctor's order.

§483.25(e)(1). *The facility must ensure that a resident who enters the facility without a limited range of motion does not experience reduction in range of motion unless the resident's clinical condition demonstrates that a reduction in range of motion is unavoidable.*

Range of motion is the degree to which your parent can extend and move her neck, arms, hands, legs, and feet. The nursing home must provide the opportunity and assistance necessary for your parent to maintain the best possible joint and muscular mobility. Range-of-motion exercises are often ordered by the doctor to prevent or restore loss of function.

§483.25(e)(2). *The facility must ensure that a resident with a limited range of motion receives appropriate treatment and services to increase range of motion and/or to prevent further decrease in range of motion.*

Your parent's care plan, if necessary, will indicate what types of exercises are needed to prevent further muscular diminution. An exercise routine will be developed and will usually fall under the guidance of the physical therapy department or the nursing assistants. If the physical therapy department is responsible for making sure these range-of-motion exercises are performed, the exercises will likely be done regularly. If the responsibility falls to the nursing assistants, however, the exercises will rarely be done. You may need to remind them, bearing in mind that the nursing assistants are the busiest of all the nursing home employees. Range-of-motion exercises are often a low priority for the nursing staff because it is busy with the most basic care tasks.

§483.25 (l) (1). *The facility must ensure that each resident's drug regimen is free from unnecessary drugs.*

The facility must prevent your parent from receiving medications that are not necessary for his or her care. I do not mean to imply that nursing home doctors or managers intentionally support the concept of medicating residents who do not need to be medicated, but since many residents complain that they "never took so many medications before arriving at the nursing home," and because some nursing home chains also own affiliated pharmacies, the possibility could exist. You should also know, however, that some residents may have neglected certain health issues before entering the facility, and those issues may need to be treated pharmacologically.

§483.25 (l) (2) (i). *The facility must ensure that residents who have not used antipsychotic drugs are not given these drugs unless antipsychotic drug therapy is necessary to treat a specific condition as diagnosed and documented in the clinical record.*

The facility is not allowed to use drugs intended to alter a resident's behavior if the intent is to subdue symptoms that are not related to a documented mental disorder. If your parent never used antipsychotic drugs before being admitted to the nursing home, and the facility now wants to initiate such drug therapy, determine the exact purpose of the medication and speak to the prescribing physician regarding this decision. Do not settle for an answer from anyone but the doctor who prescribed the medication.

I have seen countless nursing home residents prescribed antipsychotic medications with such a powerful sedative effect that the residents became zombielike, their former personalities virtually undetectable.

Sometimes these medications are given to residents who are combative and uncontrollable, but you should be aware that some facilities give these medications to subdue behaviors such as tapping, wandering, or yelling that could possibly be addressed nonpharmacologically.

If your parent must begin such drug therapy, and you notice that your parent is asleep most of the day and not eating or drinking sufficiently, the doctor should be notified. If your parent is lying in bed all day long or slumped over in a wheelchair and not frequently repositioned, you have to question whether your parent is better off without such medication. The decision to start or discontinue any medication rests with your parent or his legal representative.

You Should Know that you can request a consultation with a psychiatrist or a therapist if your parent is prescribed psychiatric medications or if she exhibits signs of mental distress. The nursing home doctor can prescribe these medications, but the facility undoubtedly has a psychiatrist on staff or available by consultation. If possible, you should seek such services from a qualified specialist.

Whoever prescribes antipsychotic medications for your parent often relies on notations in the medical record and verbal comments from the staff to determine any previous behavioral patterns. I have heard staff members deliver exaggerated reports of behavioral issues to the doctor to ensure that sedative drugs are either started or continued. To be certain that an accurate behavioral history for your parent is presented, speak to the prescribing physician about his views on behavioral treatments and the effects of the medication.

§483.25 (l) (2) (ii). *The facility must ensure that residents who use antipsychotic drugs receive gradual dose reductions, and behavioral interventions, unless clinically contraindicated, in an effort to discontinue these drugs.*

Once antipsychotic drugs have been started, the facility must monitor and attempt to gradually taper your parent off the drugs, if possible. These drugs are not supposed to be used to permanently control your parent's behavior for the convenience of the staff.

§483.60(c). *The drug regimen of each resident must be reviewed at least once a month by a licensed pharmacist.*

A licensed pharmacist must review each of the medications your parent is prescribed. After such a review the pharmacist may advise the physician that certain medications should not be given together or that a medication is being given improperly, either in dosage or in frequency.

I have seen doctors acknowledge these recommendations by signing their initials, indicating that they have reviewed the recommendation, and then make the recommended changes. I have also seen doctors review the pharmacist's recommendations but then decline to implement any changes. The object of the review is not to force the doctor to give the medications according to a specific guideline but to make the doctor aware of the pharmacist's findings.

I know of some facilities that maintain the pharmacist's written recommendations in the resident's medical chart, while others return these recommendations to the pharmacy. These records may or may not become part of your parent's permanent medical record.

§483.25(m)(2). *The facility must ensure that residents are free of any significant medication errors.*

The nursing home staff must take the necessary precautions to ensure that your parent receives the correct medication, in its correct dosage, at the correct time of day, and in the correct amount each day. A violation of any of these requirements constitutes a medication error.

You Should Know that medication errors occur frequently under a variety of circumstances. I believe the two most common types of medication errors are residents receiving the incorrect dosage of a medication because the nurse was too busy to carefully read the order, and residents receiving medications that were ordered for another resident by a nurse unfamiliar with the residents.

You can give your parent a bracelet engraved with her name and medical condition(s) to minimize the risk of her receiving another resident's medication. Many facilities have abandoned the practice of requiring residents to wear plastic identification bracelets due to their institutional nature. Instead, many facilities rely on photographs of each resident placed in the appropriate section of the nurse's medication book. As you may have guessed, the photographs are not always helpful as a resident identification tool. I have seen numerous pictures in medication books that had not been updated in several years. If your nursing home uses this method of identification, make sure the photograph of your parent is updated periodically.

Despite having an identification system in place, some nurses, especially agency nurses, use the name on the resident's door as a means of identification if they are in a hurry or if the photograph is not updated. When there are two or four people to a room, this can be a risky practice. Also, some residents get confused and lie down in a bed that is not their own.

In my opinion, the most effective way to prevent a medication error of this type is to have residents wear a name bracelet. If your facility does not use them, get one from a local jeweler or medical supply company. It need only have your parent's name for purposes of identification, but you can certainly engrave it with whatever you wish, such as "allergic to seafood" or "diabetic." You can also put your parent's name on his or her bed frame, wall, and nightstand.

§483.25 (n) (1) (ii). *The facility must develop policies and procedures that ensure that each resident is offered an influenza immunization October 1 through March 31 annually, unless the immunization is medically contraindicated or the resident has already been immunized during this time period.*

The facility must offer an influenza vaccine to your parent each year as long as his/her doctor has written an order permitting the vaccine.

§483.15 (n) (2) (ii). *The facility must develop policies and procedures that ensure that each resident is offered a pneumococcal immunization, unless the immunization is medically contraindicated or the resident has already been immunized.*

The facility must offer a pneumococcal immunization to your parent as long as his doctor has written the corresponding order.

§483.30. *The facility must have sufficient nursing staff to provide nursing and related services to attain or maintain the highest practicable physical, mental, and psychosocial well-being of each resident, as determined by resident assessments and individual plans of care.*

This is the most important regulation in the entire Nursing Home Reform Act! If this regulation were strictly followed (or enforced), nursing homes would not have such perpetually poor reputations. The domino effect of noncompliance with this requirement has made it impossible for nursing home staff to comply with most of the other regulations, which leads to an environment in which the elderly would rather not live and most nurses would rather not work.

The problem with this regulation, as it currently reads, is that it does not demand that a specific number of employees be on duty to care for a specific number of residents. Since there is no direct federal staffing requirement, facilities design their own staffing policies based on the average standard of care in the community. Basically, nursing homes compare themselves to each other, so when they are all under-performers, the bar is set quite low.

Each state is permitted to enact laws that require a specific staff-to-resident ratio, but only a handful of states have gone so far as to legislate their own staffing ratio laws.

§483.15 (f) (1). *The facility must provide for an ongoing program of activities designed to meet, in accordance with the comprehensive assessment, the interests and the physical, mental, and psychosocial well-being of each resident.*

This regulation requires the facility to provide a program of activities for all residents. The activities must appeal to each resident individually and be representative of the resident's abilities. For instance, ball tossing might be appropriate for confused residents, whereas a crossword puzzle would better suit a group of lucid, conversant residents.

If your parent enjoys being part of a group, then she will likely attend a number of activities. If your parent either does not like the activity scheduled for a particular day or prefers to do activities that require only one or two other people, then she may be alone for a large part of the day. The activity department is not usually equipped to reach the interests of all the residents as the regulation requires. I have typically seen two activity aides per one hundred residents. Do not expect to see activity personnel on duty at all times, as they are similarly under-staffed, like other positions of the nursing home.

The general theme of most activity departments is to include as many residents as possible into the largest event possible in order to meet the activity requirement. If your parent is cognitively impaired, the available opportunities for stimulating activities are few. The majority of activities are geared toward residents who function at the median level.

§483.65. *The facility must establish and maintain an infection control program designed to provide a safe, sanitary, and comfortable environment and to help prevent the development and transmission of disease and infection.*

The facility must design and implement a program that will prevent residents from acquiring and/or spreading infectious diseases like influenza, tuberculosis, scabies, and so on. The facility must keep track of residents who have a weak immune system, an invasive catheter, open sores, or increased susceptibility to contracting an infection.

§483.65 (b) (1). *When the infection control program determines that a resident needs isolation to prevent the spread of infection, the facility must isolate the resident.*

If a resident is infectious, the facility must take appropriate action to prevent the spread of infection. Usually, if a resident has an infectious disease, the protocol of choice is to place gowns, gloves, and masks outside the room so the staff can be appropriately dressed before entering. The staff members then remove and discard the disposable clothing as they exit the room. If your parent's room is designed so that adjoining rooms use the same bathroom, you should know that the residents of the adjoining room are also capable of spreading infectious germs.

It is quite common to see residents placed on infection precautions regardless of whether they have a roommate. When properly implemented, the precaution protocol is capable of preventing the spread of infection from a resident to his roommate; however, I have seen staff members gown up, enter the room, interact with the infectious resident and then, while still in their disposable garb, handle items that belong to both residents or actually touch both residents.

Another example of ineffective infection precautions is when a resident on the infection precautions is also on an alarm system, whereby the staff is alerted by a loud beep each time the resident stands. The staff member has no time to gown up before racing into the room to prevent the resident from falling and therefore cannot avoid direct, unprotected contact with the resident. He then runs the risk of infecting each resident with whom he comes in contact for the rest of his shift.

In case you are wondering why a resident with a serious infection is not immediately moved to a private room, it is because many facilities have only a few private rooms, and it is common for several residents to have a contagious disease at the same time. Rarely have I seen a facility move a resident to a private room solely to prevent the spread of infection.

§483.65 (b) (2). *The facility must prohibit employees with a communicable disease or infected skin lesions from direct contact with residents or their food, if direct contact will transmit the disease.*

The nursing home must take the necessary steps to prevent employees who are ill from passing their illnesses to the residents. You might assume that employees with contagious illnesses would not be permitted to work around the susceptible elderly, but I have found that many nursing homes are so understaffed they actually discourage employees from staying home when they are sick. I have seen staff members come to work with bronchitis, colds, sore throats, and high fevers.

I went to work one morning with a fever of 102 degrees because I knew if I did not show up the night nurse would not be able to go home. I had only slept about one hour the entire night because of a horrible cough. My plan was to relieve the night nurse and work only until the director of nurses could find a replacement. My sick time request was promptly denied because there was "absolutely no one available to finish my shift." When I said that I would, without a doubt, be absent from work the following day, the supervisor responded by saying, "Maybe if you slept in a recliner chair tonight, it would ease the cough so that you could come to work tomorrow."

Nursing home employees frequently come to work sick because they know the already understaffed nurses will have an even harder time getting all of the work done without them. There is usually no time to find a replacement when someone calls in sick with less than a twenty-four-hour notice—which is usually when an employee realizes they are not well enough to work. Employees are torn between the threat of spreading their illness and their desire to be productive team members who do not let their co-workers down by failing to show up for work. For nurses, it is often the case that one nurse cannot go home until another nurse arrives.

Also, many facilities have a policy stating that if an employee cannot come to work on a Saturday or Sunday, that employee must make up the missed shift by working on his next weekend off. Employees are usually off every other weekend. If a sick employee has important plans for the following weekend, he has no choice but to come to work while he is ill.

I once worked at a facility that required the nurse on duty to answer all calls from employees who called in sick. A form was created listing several questions to ask any employee who dared call in sick. The form included such questions as "What are your symptoms?" "Have you been to see a doctor?" "Did you receive any prescription medications?" The list included about ten questions and its intent was clearly to dissuade any employee from calling in sick. A direct quote from the form read "if symptoms are mild, encourage staff member to work at least part of their shift." We were also instructed to tell the employee that sick time would not be paid if the employee was calling in sick due to the illness of a child or other family member.

We were also told that female employees could not call in sick for any condition related to monthly menstruation. We were told that such a condition was not an illness and would not be an acceptable excuse from work. In all honesty, only about half of the nurses took that questionnaire seriously. The rest of us said, "I hope you feel better" and passed the sick call message on to management.

§483.65(b)(3). *The facility must require staff to wash their hands after each direct resident contact for which handwashing is indicated by accepted professional practice.*

Of course, this regulation has been incorporated into the policies of every nursing home. Unfortunately, however, there simply is not enough time to stop working and wash your hands after each resident contact. This is the shortcut most often taken by busy nursing home staff.

NUTRITION

§483.25(i)(1). *Based on a resident's comprehensive assessment, the facility must ensure that a resident maintains acceptable parameters of nutritional status, such as body weight and protein levels, unless the resident's clinical condition demonstrates that this is not possible.*

The facility must assess whether your parent is at risk for weight loss and/or malnutrition and, if necessary, take precautions to prevent your parent from losing weight or becoming malnourished, unless that outcome is unavoidable. There are some situations in which weight loss or malnutrition would be expected, such as chemotherapy treatments. Absent a similar scenario, the facility must prevent nutritional decline.

You Should Know if your parent is losing weight, because weight loss can indicate several things. Perhaps your parent does not like the food that she is given or maybe she needs therapeutic assistance from the nutritionist. The facility should be keeping track of how much weight your parent is gaining or losing. You should periodically ask the staff if she is gaining, losing, or maintaining, unless this information is already included in your parent's records.

Another situation that may contribute to weight loss is the fact that some residents sleep during meals. This can happen if they have been up since 4:00 a.m. or it could be due to the medication they are taking. I know of one resident who asked for a pain pill before dinner every evening and was then too tired to eat her meal. She missed dinner several nights in a row and quickly lost weight.

If your parent relies on the nursing staff to be fed his meals and if he is a slow eater, he may not be given enough time to eat his entire meal. I have seen nursing assistants feeding so many people so quickly that they get confused as to which spoon belongs to which resident. One nursing assistant actually said, "Oh, I'm sorry. That wasn't your spoon," as she removed the wrong spoon from a resident's mouth.

In situations where a resident is too tired to eat or is not willing to eat a particular meal, the staff may mark "refused" on the "check-the-box form" to show that the meal was offered but declined by the resident. The staff will offer different foods in an effort to get the resident to eat; however, if they are too busy, the form will indicate that the meal was refused.

§483.25 (i) (2). *Based on a resident's comprehensive assessment, the facility must ensure that a resident receives a therapeutic diet when there is a nutritional problem.*

The facility must provide your parent with a diet that will aid in the treatment of certain nutritional problems, usually at the direction of an order written by the doctor.

§483.25 (j). *The facility must provide each resident with sufficient fluid intake to maintain proper hydration and health.*

The facility must ensure that your parent is drinking enough fluid to prevent dehydration. If your parent cannot drink independently, the nursing home staff must assist him in consuming the appropriate amount of fluid each day. If your parent is able to drink independently, you may wish to bring him a water pitcher to keep at his bedside. Not all nursing homes provide pitchers, or, if they do, they do not keep them filled. You may need to remind the staff to keep the pitcher filled.

§483.35(a)(1). *If a qualified dietitian is not employed full-time, the facility must designate a person to serve as the director of food service who receives frequently scheduled consultations from a qualified dietitian.*

Although a dietitian is not required to be employed by the facility, one must be available for consultation. Some facilities have a dietitian who regularly visits the nursing home, while others have a dietitian on staff. In either case, you should know the name of the available dietitian and add that name to your chart in chapter 8.

§483.35(b). *The facility must employ sufficient support personnel competent to carry out the functions of the dietary service.*

The facility must have enough kitchen staff to provide each meal at the designated mealtime. But since many facilities hire the fewest possible number of people to accomplish this task, the responsibility of cleaning the dining room and collecting dirty plates, linens, and trays from the dining room usually falls to the nursing assistants. A sign of a well-staffed kitchen is when the kitchen staff is out on the nursing floors, talking to the residents, delivering food, opening sugar and jelly packets, wiping spills, and cutting food along with the nursing assistants.

If you never see the kitchen personnel mingling with the residents, that facility has hired the bare minimum of kitchen staff and is putting a burden on its already overscheduled nursing assistants. During my years as a nursing home nurse, I worked in numerous facilities where the kitchen staff never left the kitchen. When I called the kitchen for a second helping or to exchange a meal, the answer was always "Come pick it up, we don't have the staff to deliver it."

§483.35(c)(1). *Menus must meet the nutritional needs of residents in accordance with the recommended dietary allowances of the Food and*

Nutrition Board of the National Research Council, National Academy of Sciences.

The facility must serve food from all of the recommended food groups. Menus must be prepared in advance and followed.

§483.35(d)(2). *The facility must provide food that is palatable, attractive, and at the proper temperature.*

The best way to determine if a facility is complying with this regulation is to visit at mealtimes. In my experience, the dinner meal appears the least palatable and seems to contain the lowest nutritional value.

§483.35(d)(4). *The facility must provide substitutes of similar nutritional value to residents who refuse food served.*

Some facilities allow residents to choose from two entrees, while others offer a peanut butter and jelly sandwich as an alternative when the primary meal is refused. I have worked in facilities that regularly offered two main selections on the menu, but when I called the kitchen to request the alternative meal, they were "all out of" that dish just minutes after the resident received the first meal. Many facilities avoid wasting food by not preparing enough to go around.

The only way to learn the practices of your facility is to be there at mealtimes and experience the dining process for yourself.

§483.35(f)(1). *The facility must provide at least three meals daily, at regular times comparable to normal mealtimes in the community.*

You should learn the meal schedule at your facility so that you are aware of the length of time between meals. Some facilities serve the meals so close together that many residents are not hungry by the time of the next meal. Under these circumstances it would be possible for your parent to skip meals.

§483.35(f)(2). *There must be no more than fourteen hours between a substantial evening meal and breakfast the following day except as provided in (4) below.*

Many facilities allow fifteen or sixteen hours to pass between the evening meal and the breakfast meal. The evening meal is usually at 5 p.m., and the breakfast meal is usually at 8 a.m. or later. Of course, these times will vary from facility to facility.

§483.35(f)(3). *The facility must offer snacks at bedtime daily.*

Not all residents are routinely offered snacks at bedtime. Diabetic residents are supposed to receive a bedtime snack, but the snacks are not always delivered. At many facilities, the resident's name is taped onto a prepackaged snack and placed in the refrigerator. The nursing assistants are typically responsible for passing out the snacks to each diabetic or otherwise nutritionally susceptible resident. This task is often overlooked due to low staffing levels and rushed care.

I have seen labeled snacks that are outdated and undelivered. I have worked many nursing shifts during which I have asked the nursing assistants if the snacks were passed out, and many times the nursing assistants said they forgot or the residents were already asleep by the time the snacks were delivered.

I have seen very few facilities that customarily offer a substantial snack to *every* resident at bedtime. It is challenging enough to oversee that the diabetic residents are properly fed, so most facilities are not able to make evening snacks a priority for everyone.

§483.35(f)(4). *When a nourishing snack is provided at bedtime, up to sixteen hours may elapse between a substantial evening meal and breakfast the following day if a resident group agrees to this meal span, and a nourishing snack is served.*

Ask the director of nurses what types of snacks are served in the evening after the kitchen staff has gone home. The most common snacks I have seen available after normal eating hours are crackers, juice, and Jello. There should be a kitchenette on each unit where residents and their families can access snacks and drinks at any hour. Look in the refrigerator and the cabinets and determine for yourself if the kitchen is sufficiently stocked with appropriate snacks.

You Should Know that if your parent is unable to walk unassisted to the kitchenette for an evening snack, you can keep healthful, individually wrapped snacks in her room. Since few facilities offer a substantial snack in the evening, you can bring in snacks and leave instructions for the staff to deliver them to your parent each evening. You may have to call the facility and prod them into action until the task becomes routine.

§483.35(g). *The facility must provide special eating equipment and utensils for residents who need them.*

The facility must provide the necessary tools required for residents to eat their meals. If your parent needs specially shaped plates and/or eating utensils, the facility is required to provide such accommodations. Plates and utensils for residents with arthritic hands should be made available. If your parent has any difficulty eating with regular utensils, ask the director of nurses for customized utensils.

§483.35(h)(3)(i). *The facility must ensure that a feeding assistant feeds only residents who have no complicated feeding problems.*

This regulation is designed to prevent feeding assistants from feeding residents with swallowing difficulties and/or the potential for choking.

THE FACILITY MUST HAVE POLICIES AGAINST MISTREATMENT

§483.13(c). *The facility must develop and implement written policies and procedures that prohibit mistreatment, neglect, and abuse of residents and misappropriation of resident property.*

The facility must have policies in place that prohibit mistreatment, neglect, abuse, and theft. Most facilities distribute a basic version of these policies to their employees at the time they are hired.

§483.13 (c) (1) (ii) (A). *The facility must not employ individuals who have been found guilty of abusing, neglecting, or mistreating residents by a court of law.*

This regulation forbids a facility from hiring individuals who have previously been found guilty of resident abuse or neglect. Many facilities conduct a criminal background check on employees at the time they are hired to screen for any previous convictions. Each state has its own requirements for checking the background of potential employees.

You Should Know whether your facility conducts criminal background checks on its employees. You should also know whether the check is done only once, prior to hiring, or whether it is done annually. You should also determine whether a check is conducted on nursing staff only or on all employees. The facility administrator will be able to tell you what safeguards your facility has in place. If your facility does not do criminal background checks, you should insist at the next Resident Council or Family Council meeting that this procedure become a hiring prerequisite.

I know of a director of nurses who knowingly hired a nurse who had previously been penalized for theft of a resident's medications. Although you may find comfort in knowing that your facility conducts background checks (if that is the case), you may also want to know what previous charge or conviction the facility will consider acceptable in potential employees. Facilities that conduct a background check but do not consider certain crimes, like theft of residents' medications, to be grounds for refusing to hire someone should be avoided.

§483.13 (c) (1) (ii) (B). *The facility must not employ individuals who have had a finding entered into the State nurse aide registry concerning abuse, neglect, mistreatment of residents, or misappropriation of their property.*

This regulation requires the facility to check with the appropriate licensing agencies to ensure that prospective employees have not previously been found to have committed resident abuse or mistreatment.

§483.13(c)(1)(iii). *The facility must report any knowledge it has of actions by a court of law against an employee, which would indicate unfitness for service as a nurse aide or other facility staff to the State nurse aide registry or licensing authorities.*

This regulation requires nursing homes to report employee information that results from court action, if that information indicates that an employee should not work in a nursing home. The facility is required to notify the licensing agency responsible for that employee's license.

With this requirement in effect, you might think that nursing homes would not be able to hire prisoners to work inside the facility, but some facilities do in fact allow this. I once worked in a facility where prisoners worked in the kitchen department and actually hand-delivered meals to the residents.

You Should Know that if your nursing home is in the same building as, or otherwise attached to, a prison, the possibility exists that prisoners work in the facility. Ask the administrator if it is her practice to allow prisoners to work in any area of the facility. Also ask the administrator if the nursing home nurse is responsible for administering medications to the prisoners. If so, factor that information into the nurse-to-resident ratio equation.

The facility I worked at was actually attached to a prison, and the facility policy required the nurses to administer medications to a prisoner population of at least thirty, in addition to twenty-five nursing home residents! Not only did the nurse have to leave her nursing home residents to deliver medications in the prison, she had to leave every time an inmate was injured and then notify the inmate's physician and/or make the decision as to whether the inmate needed to go to the emergency room.

§483.13(c)(2). *The facility must ensure that all alleged violations involving mistreatment, neglect, or abuse, including injuries of unknown source, and misappropriation of resident property are reported immediately to the administrator of the facility and to other officials in accordance with*

State law through established procedures (including to the State survey and certification agency).

This regulation requires all nursing home staff to report violations of abuse and mistreatment (and suspected violations) to the administrator and to the appropriate state agency. Please do not assume that a complaint brought to the attention of a facility administrator has been sufficiently reported.

Based on my own experiences with facility administrators, I have found very few of them to have an authentic concern for the working conditions on each of the nursing units under their control, despite the numerous complaints that staff and residents submit regarding understaffing. Instead, I have found many of them to be fundamentally concerned with only the facility budget.

During an exit interview at a facility I'd chosen to leave, I presented the facility administrator with several typed pages listing the reasons why I felt my nursing license was in jeopardy at his facility, essentially, persistent understaffing. I was not the first nurse to have left the facility in recent months, but I was the first to actually explain my concerns cordially.

I had initially met this newly hired administrator over the telephone a few months prior to my exit interview. I had called him at home at 11:30 p.m. (his number was listed in the White Pages) to tell him I wanted to go home since my shift was over, but, as usual, a relief nurse was not scheduled. This was not the way I had intended to introduce myself to the new administrator, nor would I have phoned him had this been an isolated incident. He immediately directed a management nurse to report as my relief and assured me this would never happen again, to me or to any other nurse.

It did. It happened as regularly, as if he had never addressed the issue. Many other instances of dangerously low staffing continued to occur until I found myself sitting in his office, formal resignation in hand. I assumed he did not know what was happening since he was always tucked away in his office, seemingly unaware.

I had received quite a few shift change reports from nurses, some in tears, who had worked sixteen hours straight because a relief nurse was never scheduled and they were forced to work two shifts. The staffing problem reached the point where, prior to our shift, we would determine who the relief nurse was supposed to be and then call the nurse or agency to verify that she was, in fact, scheduled.

The facility was saving big money by arbitrarily penciling names on the schedule rather than actually paying the nursing agency to fill the gaps. Remember, an agency nurse for a night shift, especially on a weekend, would be more expensive for the facility than paying its own nurses. Some facilities do not pay nurses overtime rates for double shifts if the nurse has not yet worked forty hours that week. However, even if the facility pays the overtime rate, it is still less expensive for the facility to pay its own nurses rather than pay an agency.

My meeting with the administrator lasted approximately an hour, during which time I highlighted all of the areas where I, and many of the recently departed nurses, had concerns regarding the safety of the facility. The facility had stretched its use of MNAs to the point where the nurses were responsible for too many residents.

There were never enough staff members on duty to care for the residents, and we never knew if we were going to be able to leave at the end of our shift. The administrator said he would have the staffing issued fixed soon and that I might want to consider returning to the facility at that time.

The following year, the facility miserably failed its annual inspection as well as a follow-up inspection because it was unable to make corrective changes within the allotted time frame. The failure was so severe that the state threatened to close the facility. Local newspapers ran front-page articles of the ongoing story for several weeks. I am told that the facility is now so well staffed that its employees are tripping over each other.

My point is, formal complaints like mine can land on the desks of nursing home administrators all day long and be easily ignored. In my case, the residents who were being neglected on a daily basis were not helped until nearly a year later. My written complaint did not accomplish anything, which is why I advise you to file any complaints jointly with the administrator *and* the survey agency. In retrospect, I wish I had done this.

I know of a nurse who had a similar problem with a facility administrator. She discovered that a resident had a very large gaping wound on her backside. I saw the wound myself, because I was walking through this nurse's unit when she asked me to help her turn over the resident so she could examine a documented "reddened area" on her back. The wound was gruesome and incorrectly documented. The only existing wound documentation referenced the reddened area.

The nurse charted her findings in the resident's medical record but later noticed that her nursing notes regarding the wound had been removed from the medical chart and replaced with daily treatment notes dating back two weeks, which indicated that treatment had already begun before she had even discovered the wound. This nurse was very upset that her note had disappeared from the record. Surprisingly, all new treatment notes for the entire two-week period were in the same handwriting and signed by the same nurse.

This nurse reported to the facility administrator that her notation was missing from the resident's chart and in its place were several pages of falsified documentation from another nurse claiming the wound had been under daily treatment. The administrator said he would report the falsification of documents to the board of nursing. Months elapsed before she realized that the administrator had never reported the incident. Why would he? What would he gain besides a bad reputation for the facility? The nurse ultimately reported the incident, but the nurse who falsified the documents is still employed at the same facility.

§483.13 (c) (3). *The facility must have evidence that all alleged violations are thoroughly investigated, and must prevent further potential abuse while the investigation is in progress.*

This regulation requires the facility to have proof that the reported abuse was investigated and that steps are taken to ensure that the resident is not subject to further abuse during the investigation.

§483.13(c)(4). *The results of all investigations must be reported to the administrator or his designated representative and to other officials in accordance with state law (including to the State survey and certification agency) within 5 working days of the incident, and if the alleged violation is verified appropriate, corrective action must be taken.*

This regulation requires the facility to deliver the results of any abuse investigation to the administrator (or designated representative, usually the director of nurses) and to the appropriate state agency within five days. The facility must also take the necessary action to prevent the abuse from recurring.

THE FACILITY MUST PROVIDE A SAFE AND HOMELIKE ENVIRONMENT

§483.15(h)(1). *The facility must provide a safe, clean, comfortable, and homelike environment, allowing the resident to use his or her personal belongings to the extent possible.*

This regulation requires the facility to promote an atmosphere that resembles a home rather than an institution. The facility must make each resident's area safe, clean, and comfortable and allow the resident to use his or her own belongings whenever possible.

§483.15(h)(2). *The facility must provide housekeeping and maintenance services necessary to maintain a sanitary, orderly, and comfortable interior.*

According to this regulation, the facility must be kept clean and comfortable. Most facilities provide maintenance and housekeeping services on the day shift only. When the housekeeping staff is off duty, the cleaning responsibilities usually fall to the nursing staff. Because the nurses are so understaffed, the facility will usually be cleaner during the day shift hours.

§483.15(h)(3). *The facility must provide clean bed and bath linens that are in good condition.*

While I have never seen a facility fail to provide clean sheets, I have been to plenty of facilities that were unable to provide the sufficient number of clean towels and washcloths at bathtime.

You Should Know that many facilities require the nursing assistants to use the same washcloths for facial washing as they do for other types of washing, including cleaning fecal material off the bottoms of residents who cannot clean themselves. Disposable wipes are rarely in the budget or are limited to one or two per resident. I have seen frustrated nursing assistants use a disposable wipe to clean a resident, then fold it in half to get more use from it, then fold it in half again. The nursing assistants reported that they were only permitted to use two wipes per resident, per shift.

Most facilities use washcloths that serve the dual purpose of face cloth and diaper wipe. Some facilities dye half of their washcloths brown or another dark color to indicate that these cloths are for bottoms only. If your facility does not have a system whereby separate cloths are used for faces and bottoms, consider bringing your parent his own colored washcloths labeled with his name.

§483.15 (h) (4). *The facility must provide private closet space in each resident room.*

Although some facilities require residents to share a closet, each resident should have his or her own section of the closet.

§483.15 (h) (6). *The facility must provide comfortable and safe temperature levels. Facilities initially certified after October 1, 1990, must maintain a temperature range of 71–81 (deg) F.*

This regulation requires the facility to maintain a temperature level that is safe and comfortable for the residents regardless of the date of its initial certification. Older facilities may not be held to the same temperature standard as facilities that were certified after 1990, but all facilities must provide safe temperatures.

You Should Know whether the temperature of your parent's room is controlled within the room, by your parent, or controlled outside the room by the staff members. It is difficult for the staff to establish a comfortable temperature to all the residents, especially when anyone who so desires has access to the thermostat. Ideally, the temperature of your parent's room is within your parent's control.

When the controls are set by the staff, who are constantly moving and may prefer cooler temperatures, your parent may find the facility to be extremely chilly. I worked at a facility where repeated complaints from the residents about the cold temperatures were blatantly ignored because the staff members were too warm. Fans and air conditioners were on full blast, and many residents (and some staff members) were freezing cold in the middle of a heat wave. Residents were visibly uncomfortable and shivering.

On the other end of the spectrum, if a facility does not have air-conditioning, you should bring your parent a small air conditioner for the window of his or her room. One summer, I worked in a facility without any type of air-conditioning in the entire building. It became so hot that most of the staff members were wearing ice-packed towels around their necks as they worked. Residents were fanning themselves with papers and magazines. It was a thick, miserable heat. For me personally, it was very close to unbearable.

I saw residents lying in their beds with sweat dripping off their faces. I wiped a resident's face dry, and she was completely drenched again just minutes later. There were only a few fans in the facility that were placed in common areas and provided very little relief. Staff members were instructed to frequently offer drinks to the residents, which may have helped to avoid dehydration but did little to ease the suffering.

§483.15(h)(7). *The facility must provide for the maintenance of comfortable sound levels.*

A cordless headset can help to drown out some of the typical noise of a busy nursing home, especially if your parent's room is near the nurse's station or if he or she has a roommate with frequent visitors.

§483.25 (h) (1). *The facility must ensure that the resident environment remains as free of accident hazards as is possible.*

The facility must utilize equipment that is safe and must take necessary action to prevent accidents and injuries.

You Should Know whether your parent's facility is equipped with indoor water sprinklers that would be activated in the event of a fire. All nursing homes have a fire evacuation plan, but not all nursing homes have automatic sprinklers in the ceilings. After several tragic nursing home fires in recent years, some states have required nursing homes to install sprinklers.

§483.25 (h) (2). *The facility must ensure that each resident receives adequate supervision and assistance devices to prevent accidents.*

Your parent's initial and periodic assessments should identify whether your parent is at risk for falling or otherwise injuring himself. Not only should the nursing home staff recognize the risk of such an injury, the facility must be adequately staffed and take appropriate measures to prevent foreseeable accidents.

Specifically, this would include supervision of residents while they are assisted to and from the bathroom. I have seen countless injuries occur because the resident was left in the bathroom while the nursing assistant left to help another resident. The resident would usually tire of waiting, push her call button, and eventually attempt to leave the bathroom alone when she was not physically capable of doing so.

§483.70 (h) (4). *The facility must maintain an effective pest control program so that the facility is free of pests and rodents.*

The facility must recognize and eliminate pest infestations within the facility.

CHAPTER 5

NURSING HOME INSPECTIONS

"I love working when the state is here.
We always have all the staff we need."
—a nursing assistant during a three-day nursing home inspection

The Nursing Home Reform Act requires facilities that accept Medicaid and Medicare reimbursement payments to undergo regular inspections of the facility to ensure compliance with the laws set forth in the act. Each state has a designated agency in charge of inspecting the facilities within its jurisdiction. As previously mentioned, the contact information for the agency charged with conducting these inspections must be posted in your facility.

The state survey agency is responsible for inspecting nursing homes in several situations. To illustrate how the most common type of nursing home inspection is conducted, this chapter deals primarily with the annual inspection, even though there are other types of nursing home inspections.

TYPES OF INSPECTIONS

Nursing homes are subject to annual inspections, follow-up inspections, and inspections that are conducted in response to complaints filed with the agency. Despite the term *annual inspection*, nursing homes are usually inspected every twelve to eighteen months. This type of inspection is typically performed during the same time frame each year, usually on a weekday. Inspectors occasionally stay into the evening so they can conduct part of their investigation on the later shift. They rarely show up in the middle of the night or on weekends.

A follow-up inspection is conducted when a facility has failed a previous inspection and corrective action was needed to rectify a failing grade and/or an environment deemed potentially dangerous for residents. This inspection is conducted to ascertain whether the facility has appropriately identified and completed the necessary action to bring the facility into the realm of compliance.

An inspection will also take place if a complaint is filed with the inspecting agency and it is determined that the complaint warrants the additional inspection. For instance, inspectors may perform an additional inspection to investigate specific allegations of abuse, neglect, or mistreatment, or in response to general complaints of poor care.

Complaints may be made by residents' family members, facility staff members, or anyone with knowledge of or suspicions that a facility is not in compliance with regulations, resulting in the potential to place residents in harm's way. In order to verify such allegations, the agency will usually conduct some form of investigation, which may include an additional inspection.

You Should Know that since many complaints are received through the state ombudsman's office, this office may be able to supply you with additional information regarding your nursing home. The ombudsman's office acts as a resident advocate whose main concern is the safety and well-being of nursing home residents. Some offices will share information regarding recent complaints, while other offices are more discreet regarding the release of such information.

Most states allow volunteers to work with the ombudsman's office to assist in investigating complaints. If you choose to volunteer your time, this may be another way for you to learn about nursing homes and, particularly, the nursing home where your parent resides. The contact information for your state ombudsman's office must be posted in every facility.

HOW THE FACILITY PREPARES FOR THE ANNUAL INSPECTION

Passing the annual inspection is vital to the reputation and survival of every nursing home. It is often the most important aspect of a nursing home manager's job. The facility administrator knows in advance when the annual inspection is to take place (usually the same month each year) and so is able to prepare.

With advance notice of the impending inspection, facility managers are able to prepare themselves and staff members for the arrival of the inspectors. Management attire is upgraded, rumors circulate about the exact arrival date of the inspectors, and a higher stress level is undeniable. Even the nurses and nursing assistants are nervous about the upcoming inspection because they do not want to be the reason the facility receives a deficient mark. It is common knowledge that the inspectors attentively watch the nurses and nursing assistants for a period of time as they deliver care. Anyone whose actions cause a failing mark is the subject of unfavorable gossip for months. I cannot count the number of times I heard the painful details recapitulated. "Jane didn't even change her gloves between residents and the inspector saw the whole thing." "The inspector saw her use a gauze bandage that had been dropped on the floor." "We failed that part because Jane did not document properly."

With personal reputations at stake, each staff member is motivated to do his job as efficiently as possible. How can nurses and nursing assistants perform flawless work in the presence of the inspectors when they do not have enough time or staff to do it properly in their absence? The nursing home managers make certain that during the period inspectors may arrive, employees and needed supplies are plentiful.

I recall working at a facility that was out of supplies on a regular basis. By supplies, I mean plastic cups to give water with pills, plastic spoons for the administration of crushed or liquid medications, gloves, tissues, and gauze bandages for wound care. On several occasions, we had to send an employee to the local grocery store with our own money (which was later reimbursed) to get the supplies the facility failed to furnish! I was frustrated by these instances countless times during the course of the year, yet I never witnessed a shortage of supplies during the inspection period. I saw only the opposite. The director and administrator nearly tripped over each other to offer assistance and fetch supplies for the nursing staff when the inspectors were onsite.

The facility also makes sure that the medical records are up to date before the inspectors' arrival. For instance, most facilities hire a nurse whose sole job is to search through the medical records to make sure nothing is out of compliance. If she finds something, such as a nursing note that needs an addendum or a care plan entry that has not been executed, she brings it to the attention of the director so it can be rectified prior to the anticipated inspection date.

Many facilities conduct what is known as a "mock inspection," whereby nurses who have experience with state inspections are hired to conduct a simulated inspection. This gives the facility an idea of how they will fare during the actual inspection, which may still be months away. The necessary improvements are implemented to ensure the desired survey result.

For weeks in advance of the inspection, the director of nurses randomly selects employees for questioning during the workday. "Where's the closest fire extinguisher?" "What is our policy for catheter care?" "What should you do if you see that a resident has fallen?" The staff members are prepared to answer any question that the inspectors may ask.

There are also a multitude of books, magazines, and manuals available to the director intended to prepare nursing home management for the annual inspection. The inspection is treated as a three-day clinical test for which the facility must study and then pass. By studying for the test a director can improve the facility's score.

Some facilities require staff members to attend seminars, often conducted by state inspectors, which let the facility management know how to avoid a deficient mark in each area of the inspection. I attended one such seminar at the request of my supervising director of nurses. The speaker, a current state inspector at the time, said that his eyebrow was raised each time he read in a resident's medical chart the word *bruise*. The definition of *bruise*, he noted, is the result of an injury. Therefore, every time he read the word *bruise* he had to dig further to determine whether an injury had occurred. My director immediately whispered to us, "Let's not use the word 'bruise' anymore; document in other terms such as 'discoloration.' Let all the other nurses know."

My point is that a director can become adept at test taking by knowing what the inspector will be looking for and by mastering preparation techniques. Although most inspections are extremely thorough, a facility can improve its inspection results without improving the care of its residents.

THE NURSING HOME INSPECTION PROCESS

Prior to their arrival at the facility, the inspectors have gathered necessary information about their subject. They have reviewed previous inspection results to determine if the facility has any sort of citation pattern. They have reviewed any complaints that may have been reported to the state ombudsman's office. If the facility has recently been mentioned in the newspaper regarding an adverse event, that event is reviewed prior to the inspection.

Once the inspectors arrive at the facility, they conduct an entrance conference. The team of inspectors, usually three to five, meets with the administrator and announces that the inspection is about to begin. The inspectors request information such as written policies and procedures, mealtimes, and staffing information. They post a sign near the entrance to the facility to alert visitors that an inspection is in progress.

The inspectors assign themselves to the many areas of the facility that require inspection. They check cleanliness, including the kitchen and dining areas; they observe and speak to residents; they observe an entire medication pass to ensure compliance with physician orders and federal regulations; they inspect the building for compliance with building codes; they observe eating and feeding practices; and they monitor wound care technique and procedures.

The process of inspecting the entire facility usually takes three to five days, depending on the size and condition of the facility. During this time the facility managers are at the beck and call of the inspectors, fielding questions and supplying documentation. The management staff is more visible than usual and is extremely accommodating to both inspectors and nursing staff.

It is critical that the number of staff on duty be higher than usual because the facility managers do not want the inspectors to know that they are usually understaffed. They want a smooth and uneventful inspection to yield passing results. In order to achieve that end, they help feed residents, beef up the staff, answer telephones, answer call bells, and even go into residents' rooms to assist them.

You Should Know that you will not get a realistic view of the nursing home if you judge it during a state inspection. The dining process may be more pleasant, the staff-to-resident ratio will be more manageable, and the facility will be cleaner and smell fresher than normal. If you can visit during an inspection and again during regular hours, I urge you to note and report the differences between routine care and care delivered during the inspection process.

While the inspection process is a stressful time for the employees, it is also a relief for the nursing assistants who finally get the help they need to do their job properly. Throughout every nursing home inspection I have witnessed, the nursing assistants have voiced gratitude for the extra help that miraculously arrives during these critical days.

As part of the inspection, a group of people is selected to speak privately with the inspectors regarding the care of the residents. The group often includes residents' family members and staff members. They are individually and anonymously asked questions about the treatment of the residents and whether they have personally witnessed any abuse or mistreatment. The chosen individuals have the opportunity to offer the inspectors any information that might be helpful to the investigative process.

At the end of the inspection, inspectors analyze all the information they have collected. For each area of the inspection in the facility failed to meet the legal requirements, a deficiency is issued. Each deficiency is broken into two parts: severity and scope.

A deficiency is categorized as one of four possible levels of severity. A level-1 deficiency is the lowest grade and is characterized as having the potential to cause harm to residents, while a level-4 deficiency is the highest and worst grade, requiring the facility to implement an emergency plan of correction to avoid imminent danger to its residents.

The scope of the deficiency refers to the number of residents affected by the deficiency. A deficiency can affect as few as one or two residents or it can be a widespread deficiency affecting every resident in the facility.

The final part of the inspection process is the exit conference. The administrator and other members of management meet with the inspectors at the conclusion of the final day of the inspection. During this meeting, the deficiencies issued against the facility are disclosed.

INTERPRETATION OF THE ANNUAL INSPECTION RESULTS

The results of all Centers for Medicare- and Medicaid-mandated nursing home inspections are available at http://www.medicare.gov. You can also obtain a copy of the inspection results directly from the survey agency in your state or by asking your facility administrator.

To show you an example of annual inspection results, I have included below various figures from the online results of a nursing home in Massachusetts. I have never been to this facility, so we are looking at this information without any firsthand knowledge.

You will notice in figure 1 that the first column includes the identifying information of the facility. The next column indicates whether the facility accepts Medicare (skilled care), Medicaid (long-term care), or both and the initial date of certification. The next column indicates that this is a not-for-profit facility, has one hundred beds, and is not located within a hospital. This facility does not provide continuing care retirement living according to the information in the fourth column. Such facilities have retirement housing, assisted-living accommodations, and varied levels of care to meet the continued needs of its residents. The last column indicates that this facility has both a Resident Council and a Family Council already in place.

Figure 1

Name: _____
Address: _____
Phone
Number: _____
Date of last
  Change of
  Ownership _____
	Medicare
	Participation
	Initial Date
	of
	Certification
	Medicaid
	Partiticpation
		Type of
		Ownership
		Total Number
		of Certified
		Beds
		Located
		in a
		Hospital
			Continuing
			Care
			Retirement
			Community
				Resident
				and Family
				Councils

Long-Term Care XXXX Road XXXX, MA XXXXX (555) 555–5555 Month/Day/Year	Yes ———— 01/01/1967 ———— Yes	Nonprofit Corporation 100 ———— No	No	Both

Figure 2 shows the facility's staffing data. The columns are divided into three categories. The first column shows the amount of nursing time the facility provides each resident each day. This facility reports one hour and thirty-eight minutes of licensed nursing staff hours per resident per day. The second column shows that the average nursing time per resident per day in the state of Massachusetts is two hours and six minutes, and in the third column, the national average is shown: one hour and thirty minutes.

In my opinion, the staffing data provided by the facility is misleading because it would be incorrect to assume that each resident at this facility receives over one and a half hours of *exclusive* nursing care each day. The facility arrives at this figure by dividing the number of nursing hours in the facility by the number of residents in the facility.

A nurse who spends much of her time in an office but delivers some nursing care may be factored into this equation, inappropriately adding eight hours of nursing care and resulting in a skewed figure.

In a facility that accepts skilled-care residents, like this facility, you can be sure that most of the nursing hours are dedicated to treating the skilled-care residents because they are usually more dependent on the staff than the long-term-care residents.

In my opinion, there is no way to accurately measure the number of nursing or nursing assistant hours per resident per day short of following your parent all day and pressing a stopwatch each time he receives nursing care. Use the information provided in this section as a guide, not as a way to calculate the actual staffing ratio.

Figure 2

Nursing Homes and/or Skilled Nursing Facilities Located Within Continuing Care Retirement Communities for residents needing short or long stay			
Nursing Staff Hours Per Resident Per Day, is the average daily hours worked by the nurses or nursing assistants divided by total number of residents. The amount of care given to each resident varies.			
	LONG-TERM CARE	**State Average in Massachusetts**	**National Average**
Number of Residents	73	65.2	77.1
Licensed Nursing Staff:			
Registered Nurses Hours	51 minutes	1 hour 6 minutes	42 minutes
Licensed Practical Nurses/Licensed Vocational Nurses Hours	+ 47 minutes	+ 1 hour	+ 48 minutes
Total Number of Licensed Nursing Staff Hours	= 1 hour 38 minutes	= 2 hours 6 minutes	= 1 hour 30 minutes
Certified Nursing Assistants Hours	2 hours 31 minutes	2 hours 48 minutes	2 hours 42 minutes

Figure 3, below, lists the contact information for the long-term-care ombudsman's office and the State Survey Agency.

Figure 3

Long-Term Care Ombudsman	1-800-243-4636
State Survey Agency	Massachusetts Department of Public Health 1-800-462-5540

Figure 4 illustrates how the inspection results from this nursing home compare to other nursing homes in Massachusetts and to the national average. Notice that the seventh row shows that this nursing home was found to have 22 percent of its long-term residents physically restrained, while the average for this practice in Massachusetts and nationally is only 5 percent. In the thirteenth row, you will see that 16 percent of long-term-care residents were found to have a urinary tract infection, compared with a national average of 9 percent.

Figure 4

Quality Measures	Percentage for LONG-TERM CARE	Average in Massachusetts	National Average
Percent of Long-Stay Residents Given Influenza Vaccination during the Flu Season NEW!	96%	89%	88%
Percent of Long-Stay Residents Who Were Assessed and Given Pneumococcal Vaccination NEW!	84%	85%	83%
Percent of Long-Stay Residents Whose Need for Help with Daily Activities Has Increased	17%	15%	15%
Percent of Long-Stay Residents Who Have Moderate to Severe Pain	2%	3%	4%

Figure 4 (continued)

Quality Measures	Percentage for LONG-TERM CARE	Average in Massachusetts	National Average
Percent of High-Risk Long-Stay Residents Who Have Pressure Sores	NOT AVAILABLE	11%	12%
Percent of Low-Risk Long-Stay Residents Who Have Pressure Sores	NOT AVAILABLE	2%	2%
Percent of Long-Stay Residents Who Were Physically Restrained	22%	5%	5%
Percent of Long-Stay Residents Who Are More Depressed or Anxious	15%	15%	14%
Percent of Low-Risk Long-Stay Residents Who Lose Control of Their Bowels or Bladder	NOT AVAILABLE	61%	49%
Percent of Long-Stay Residents Who Have/Had a Catheter Inserted and Left in Their Bladder	0%	5%	6%
Percent of Long-Stay Residents Who Spend Most of Their Time in Bed or in a Chair	3%	2%	4%
Percent of Long-Stay Residents Whose Ability to Move about In and Around Their Room Got Worse	NOT AVAILABLE	14%	12%
Percent of Long-Stay Residents with a Urinary Tract Infection	16%	10%	9%
Percent of Long-Stay Residents Who Lose Too Much Weight	9%	7%	8%

Figure 4 (continued)

Quality Measures	Percentage for LONG-TERM CARE	Average in Massachusetts	National Average
Percent of Short-Stay Residents Given Influenza Vaccination during the Flu Season NEW!	90%	78%	77%
Percent of Short-Stay Residents Who Were Assessed and Given Pneumococcal Vaccination NEW!	NOT AVAILABLE	77%	74%
Percent of Short-Stay Residents with Delirium	NOT AVAILABLE	2%	2%
Percent of Short-Stay Residents Who Had Moderate to Severe Pain	NOT AVAILABLE	20%	21%
Percent of Short-Stay Residents with Pressure Sores	NOT AVAILABLE	15%	16%

The fourth row of figure 5 shows that the facility's total number of health deficiencies was only one. The national average is shown as eight. The last row of the chart shows that the deficiency was issued because the facility failed to "write and use policies that forbid mistreatment, neglect and abuse of residents and theft of residents' property." The facility corrected the deficiency on September 7, 2006. The deficiency was found to be a level-1, which affected many residents.

The same format is used to illustrate the facility's seven fire/safety deficiencies in figure 6 on page 160. Notice that this facility has sprinkler systems. The average number of fire/safety violations in Massachusetts is one, while the national average is three. This facility was cited for not having

1. corridor and hallway doors that block smoke
2. proper stairway enclosures and vertical shafts
3. construction that can resist fire for one hour or an approved fire extinguishing system

4. a record of quarterly fire drills for each shift under varying conditions

5. an approved installation, maintenance and testing program for fire alarm systems

6. an approved automatic sprinkler system connected to the fire alarm system

7. automatic sprinkler systems that have been maintained in working order

All corrections were made October 23, 2006.

Figure 5

LONG-TERM CARE XXXXXXX ROAD XXXXXXX, MA XXXXX (555) 555-5555	
Date of last standard health inspection:	08/23/2006
Quality Indicator Survey	No
Dates of Complaint Investigations:	09/01/2006–11/30/2007
Total number of health deficiencies for this nursing home:	1
Average number of health deficiencies in Massachusetts:	6
Average number of health deficiencies in the United States:	8
Range of health deficiencies in Massachusetts:	0–40
View Previous Inspection Results	

Mistreatment Deficiencies			
Inspectors determined that the nursing home failed to:	**Date of Correction**	**Level of Harm (Least -> Most)**	**Residents Affected (Few -> Some -> Many)**
1. Write and use policies that forbid mistreatment, neglect and abuse of residents and theft of residents' property. (08/23/2006)	09/07/2006	1 = Potential for minimal harm	Many

Figure 6

LONG-TERM CARE XXXXXXXXX ROAD XXXXXXXXX MA XXXXX (555) 555-5555	
Automatic Sprinkler Systems in All Required Areas	Fully Sprinklered
Date of last standard fire safety inspection:	09/11/2006
Dates of Complaint Investigations:	09/01/2006–11/30/2007
Total number of fire safety deficiencies for this nursing home:	7
Average number of fire safety deficiencies in Massachusetts:	1
Average number of fire safety deficiencies in the United States:	3
Range of fire safety deficiencies in Massachusetts:	0–13
View Previous Inspection Results	

Corridor Walls and Doors Deficiencies			
Inspectors determined that the building did not have	**Date of Correction**	**Level of Harm (Least -> Most)**	**Residents Affected (Few -> Some -> Many)**
1. corridor and hallway doors that block smoke (09/11/2006)	10/23/2006	1 = Potential for minimal harm	Many

Vertical Openings Deficiencies			
Inspectors determined that the building did not have	**Date of Correction**	**Level of Harm (Least -> Most)**	**Residents Affected (Few -> Some -> Many)**
2. proper stairway enclosures and vertical shafts (09/11/2006)	10/23/2006	2 = Minimal harm or potential for actual harm	few

Hazardous Area Deficiencies			
Inspectors determined that the building did not have	**Date of Correction**	**Level of Harm (Least -> Most)**	**Residents Affected (Few -> Some -> Many)**
3. construction that can resist fire for one hour or an approved fire extinguishing system (09/11/2006)	10/23/2006	2 = Minimal harm or potential for actual harm	Few
Emergency Plans and Fire Drills Deficiencies			
Inspectors determined that the building did not have	**Date of Correction**	**Level of Harm (Least -> Most)**	**Residents Affected (Few -> Some -> Many)**
4. record of quarterly fire drills for each shift under varying conditions (09/11/2006)	10/23/2006	1 = Potential for minimal harm	Many
Fire Alarm Systems Deficiencies			
Inspectors determined that the building did not have	**Date of Correction**	**Level of Harm (Least -> Most)**	**Residents Affected (Few -> Some -> Many)**
5. an approved installation, maintenance and and testing program for fire alarm systems (09/11/2006)	10/23/2006	1 = Potential for minimal harm	Many

Automatic Sprinkler Systems Deficiencies			
Inspectors determined that the building did not have	Date of Correction	Level of Harm (Least -> Most)	Residents Affected (Few -> Some -> Many)
6. an approved automatic sprinkler system connected to the fire alarm system (09/11/2006)	10/23/2006	2 = Minimal harm or potential for actual harm	Few
7. automatic sprinkler systems that have been maintained in working order (09/11/2006)	10/23/2006	1 = Potential for minimal harm	Many

Figure 7 shows the number of deficiencies for the three previous inspections for this facility. Note the dates of the prior inspections, which all occurred within the same three-week range.

Figure 7

Deficiency Category	Survey Date: 08/23/2006 Complaint Reporting Period: 08/01/2006– 10/31/2007	Survey Date: 09/12/2005 Complaint Reporting Period: 08/01/2005– 7/31/2006	Survey Date 09/15/2004 Complaint Reporting Period: 08/01/2004– 7/31/2005
Mistreatment	1	0	0
Quality Care	0	1	1
Resident Assessment	0	3	0
Resident Rights	0	0	0
Nutrition and Dietary	0	1	0
Pharmacy Service	0	1	0
Environmental	0	0	0
Administration	0	1	0
Reported Between Inspections	0	0	0

To highlight the issue of predictability for annual inspection dates, notice the dates of three consecutive annual inspections of a Nevada nursing home (figure 8) and a North Dakota nursing home (figure 9).

Figure 8

Deficiency Category	Survey Date: 05/15/2007 Complaint Reporting Period: 08/01/2006– 10/31/2007	Survey Date: 05/23/2006 Complaint Reporting Period: 08/01/2005– 7/31/2006	Survey Date 06/23/2005 Complaint Reporting Period: 08/01/2004– 7/31/2005
Mistreatment	0	1	0
Quality Care	2	6	4
Resident Assessment	0	2	2
Resident Rights	0	2	3
Nutrition and Dietary	0	0	1
Pharmacy Service	0	0	1
Environmental	0	1	3
Administration	0	2	0
Reported Between Inspections	0	0	0

Figure 9

Deficiency Category	Survey Date: 08/30/2007 Complaint Reporting Period: 08/01/2006– 10/31/2007	Survey Date: 08/10/2006 Complaint Reporting Period: 08/01/2005– 7/31/2006	Survey Date 08/18/2005 Complaint Reporting Period: 08/01/2004– 7/31/2005
Mistreatment	0	0	0
Quality Care	2	3	1
Resident Assessment	0	0	0
Resident Rights	0	1	1
Nutrition and Dietary	0	0	0
Pharmacy Service	3	0	0
Environmental	3	1	1
Administration	0	0	0
Reported Between Inspections	0	0	0

You should collect the previous inspection results for your facility to see how the facility has performed in each area. You will also be able to determine when the annual inspection typically occurs. If you have any questions regarding any of the inspection results, you should contact the director of nurses or the survey agency.

CHAPTER 6

IMPROVING NURSING HOME LIFE

"It's not wet enough."
—a nursing assistant reporting that she could not change a resident's
soiled diaper due to a policy that prevented her from changing a diaper
until at least half of the stripes on the outside changed color

This chapter is a compilation of suggestions and advice that aims to directly improve the quality of nursing home life for your parent. These suggestions address many of the common complaints I have heard while visiting in or working in nursing homes. Some of these tips are very simple and require very little effort, yet they may make a significant impact on whether or not your parent is satisfied with nursing home living.

ASK FOR SPECIAL TREATMENT

In every nursing home there are a few residents who receive preferential treatment. A resident may be well known in the community or have a relative who works in the facility, and based on that status, he or she may receive more attentive care. I have worked in a few facilities where the parent of the administrator was a resident. It was made emphatically clear that when that resident's call bell rang, staff members were to answer it immediately.

Do not be afraid to ask the nursing staff for anything your parent might need. For the large majority of residents, if family members do not make special requests on their behalf, their treatment will rarely be above mediocre or, more often, above inadequate.

You might need to make a special request if your parent loses personal items on a regular basis. Some lost items can cost hundreds of dollars to replace. Hearing aids are among the most expensive (and most common) items lost by residents. If you do not ask the nursing staff to monitor the location of these items, they will not voluntarily take it upon themselves to do so.

Regardless of your parent's diagnosis or abilities, hearing aids should be engraved with initials or some other mark of identification. You should also periodically check to see whether your parent is wearing his own hearing aid or one that belongs to another resident. All nursing home staff who assist residents with hearing aids occasionally get them mixed up, and residents are often found wearing hearing aids that belong to other residents.

You Should Know that if your parent loses his hearing aid, the facility may be financially responsible for its replacement. Residents lose their hearing aids in their bedding, on their meal trays, and during their appointments outside of the facility. If the hearing aid is not found, the nursing home may be responsible for replacing it if the staff was responsible for its loss.

If your parent is incapable of maintaining his own hearing aid, you should insist that the staff be accountable for its whereabouts. If the staff maintains control of the hearing aids, the nurses keep them in a locked area and sign a form each morning to indicate that they have given the hearing aids to the residents. Every evening the nurse signs that she has retrieved all of the hearing aids from the residents and returned them to the locked area.

If a hearing aid is lost under these circumstances, it is usually the fault of the staff and not the resident. I have seen many facilities foot the bill for a new hearing aid if this happens. If your parent frequently removes his hearing aid and leaves it in various places, you should ask the staff to keep it during the night. You should ask for this arrangement for any medical item that might be lost and would be expensive to replace, such as eyeglasses or dentures if your parent cannot keep track of these items.

If your parent is able to maintain control of his own personal items, it is best not to mix them with those of the other residents. Some items are best left in your parent's room where he can be certain they are not accidentally given to other residents. Bring in a bedside table that has a locking drawer if the facility has not provided your parent with a secure storage area.

You Should Know that if your parent's eyedrops, inhalers, and nasal sprays are stored on the medication cart along with those of other residents, the possibility exists that other residents may be using the same bottles and vials. Eyedrops, inhalers, and nasal sprays are normally labeled with each resident's name and are intended for individual use since the container usually touches the resident's eyes, mouth, and nose with each use. The bottles and vials are often stored in one large compartmentalized drawer but very often get mixed together.

I have seen many nurses accidentally (or intentionally) use the eyedrops, inhalers, and nasal sprays that belong to one resident on another resident who is without that medication. Often a resident is without medication if the pharmacy did not receive the order or if it was simply not reordered when the bottle ran out. Often residents receive medication that belongs to another resident until their own refill arrives.

I have also seen many of these "community" drawers that contain the inhalers of residents who have serious, contagious infections, yet all of the inhalers and sprays are touching each other. Remember, you will need a doctor's order to allow your parent to store any medication in his or her room.

Many nursing homes routinely operate with old and faulty equipment that is in a constant state of disrepair. You may find that showers, tubs, mechanical lifts, wheelchairs, and beds are not always operable. Beds that are raised and lowered manually are sometimes missing the handles to elevate the head or foot section.

You Should Know whether your parent's bed is electrical or manual and whether it is currently operable. If it is electrical, make sure your parent knows how to raise the head and foot of the bed so she does not need to wait for a staff member to respond to her call bell. If the bed is manual, your parent will probably have to use the call bell each time she wants to have it adjusted. I have seen many residents with older manual beds that do not function. The head and foot of the bed could not be raised. Many residents need the foot of the bed raised in order to elevate swollen feet, and they need the head of the bed raised when they are eating or taking medication.

Many facilities have both electrical and manual beds. If your parent currently has a manual bed and would like an electrical bed, check to see if any are available and if you can make a switch. You may have to wait before an electrical model becomes available, but you should insist on your parent having an operable bed.

Another common complaint from nursing home residents is that their mattress is uncomfortable. I have heard countless residents say, "This is the most uncomfortable bed I have ever had." The mattresses provided by the facility are not usually the name brands that promise comfort and a great night's sleep.

To help your parent with this issue, you can either buy a higher-quality mattress or add a foam mattress pad to the mattress. Some facilities have foam mattress toppers stored on the premises, but many do not provide them to the residents unless they are requested.

IMPROVING THE QUALITY OF LIFE

The nursing home is the place your parent now calls home, even if it is only a temporary stay. You want to be sure that she is living comfortably.

In order to help your parent realize that goal, you should learn as much about the facility as possible.

You Should Know if the facility has a pet and whether your parent likes or dislikes the idea of having a pet in her living area. Many facilities have cats, birds, fish, or dogs for the residents to enjoy. Some residents are thrilled to be around any type of pet, while others are allergic or uninterested. If your parent does not want the facility mascot in her room, relay that request to the facility administrator. I worked in a facility whose resident cat bit and scratched numerous residents. After several complaints, the cat was finally given to a staff member to take home.

Residents are usually permitted to have fish or other very small pets in their rooms. You could also attach a bird feeder to the outside of your parent's window or to a nearby tree so that he is able to get a close view of the birds. You may need to ask the activity department to keep it filled if your parent is not able to maintain it himself. Many facilities also allow family members to bring their pets in for visits with the residents. Check with the administrator to find out the pet policy at your facility.

You Should Know that you will learn more about the facility if you visit at odd hours and on weekends than if you visit strictly during the day. In order for you to get an accurate picture of what the facility is really like, you will need to visit at times when visitors are not usually expected. You want to learn how your parent is doing at various points during the day, and in order to do that, you should stagger the times of your visits. For instance, you could visit at 5 a.m. one day, 3 p.m. the next day, and 9 p.m. the following evening. The key is to step outside of your normal visiting routine and avoid visiting at the same time each day.

Remember, weekends are the most understaffed days of the week because that is when most workers call in sick and when the facility is already minimally staffed. If you want to get an idea of how your facility operates when it is understaffed, this would be the time to visit. The facility also experiences frequent staffing shortages on the evening shift.

The building will probably be locked during the very early and very late hours. Some facilities allow visitors to use a building code to enter the building after hours, while others require visitors to use a buzzer system with a video camera fixed on the entryway. I have heard complaints from many family members who say they have stood outside for extremely long periods of time while waiting for a staff member to buzz them into the building. If you encounter any difficulty entering the building after hours, speak to the administrator about getting in through an alternate entrance or ask for the building code.

It would be easier for you to learn the various practices of the nursing home if you had the help of another person who already regularly visits the facility. You could take turns visiting at the very early and very late hours.

You Should Know that if you befriend another resident's family member, the two of you can work as a team to get better care for both of your parents. I firmly believe that residents who have family members actively involved in their care really do receive better services. If you get involved in the care of another resident, and her family becomes involved in the care of your parent, you will double the visitation time your parents receive and you will have an extra set of eyes on each parent, checking for wetness, cleanliness, and overall well-being. The staff will know that these residents have serious advocates. An alliance with another family member will make both your jobs easier.

In order to meet another family member with whom you can join forces, attend or initiate the Family Council meetings. There is a chart in chapter 8 that will help you keep track of all of the members. You might also meet a prospective partner while visiting your parent. Take the opportunity to introduce yourself to other visitors each time you visit the facility. Find out if there are other visitors who are equally as motivated to get good care for their parents.

Privacy laws do not prohibit you from visiting another resident who agrees to your company, nor do they prevent you from pointing out to the nursing assistant that he has had the call light on for ten minutes and needs help to the bathroom. Of course, you will not be able to review the medical record of other residents.

Another important factor to consider when evaluating your parent's comfort level is whether or not he and his roommate are well suited. Ideally your parent will have a roommate whose needs and abilities are similar to his own.

You Should Know the compatibility of your parent's roommate because nursing home managers do not always put a great deal of thought into placing compatible residents in the same room. If your parent is oriented to his surroundings and able to get to the bathroom independently, he should not be rooming with someone who requires a nurse to come in every few hours during the night for changing and repositioning, which usually involves turning on the lights and waking both residents. Nor should your parent room with someone who constantly yells or moans if your parent would be disturbed by those behaviors.

If your parent is in a room with a resident whose medical needs are a constant source of interruption to your parent's routine, you should alert the administrator and demand another living arrangement.

You Should Know the number of people who share the bathroom in your parent's room and whether your parent is frequently inconvenienced by the situation. This issue has been the source of many complaints from residents who share bathrooms. Most facilities are designed with shared bathrooms, and residents typically share a bathroom with at least one other resident. However, a bathroom can also be situated between two rooms, and all the occupants of both rooms may share a single bathroom.

A common complaint I have heard from residents who share a bathroom with more than one person is that someone is always in the bathroom and that it is never available when needed. If your parent is able to use a common bathroom in another area of the facility, she may prefer that rather than waiting for her own bathroom to become vacant. Your parent may otherwise choose to move to another room with fewer occupants per bathroom.

A more frequent complaint among residents who share a bathroom with multiple people is that their bathroom is never clean. If your parent shares a bathroom and has complaints about cleanliness, ask the housekeeping manager to have the bathroom cleaned more often than the typical one cleaning a day.

You Should Know that if your parent is a smoker, the facility probably has policies that limit the number of times a day she can smoke. Your parent may have to leave the building and go to a designated outdoor smoking area. Depending on the level of supervision your parent requires, she may need a staff member to accompany her each time she wants to smoke a cigarette. Ask the director of nurses about the terms of the facility's policy and how your parent will get the necessary supervision.

GETTING BETTER NURSING CARE

As you have learned, it is hard to get good nursing care when the staffing levels are low, but there are a few more things you can do to improve poor care and reduce your parent's chances of having an accident.

Many deaths and serious injuries occur each winter when elderly residents leave the building unnoticed and wander away. Sometimes residents die in the cold before they are found by staff members. You should ask the director of nurses what type of prevention system is in place to protect your parent from this type of tragedy.

You Should Know whether your facility is equipped with an alarm system that will alert staff members in the event your parent leaves the building unaccompanied. Most facilities have exit doors that are equipped with an alarm system that is triggered when a resident wearing an activated bracelet attempts to exit the building. If your parent's diagnosis involves any type of mental confusion, you can ask the staff to apply a bracelet to your parent's ankle or wheelchair to prevent him from wandering out of the building.

If your facility does not have any safety procedures in place to prevent such an occurrence, you should immediately discuss the issue with the Family Council members and the administrator. If the administrator chooses not to install a safety mechanism on the exit doors, consider moving your parent to another facility if he is at risk of wandering off on his own.

So many nursing home chains report enormous annual profits that it is hard to believe that the residents who generate these huge investment returns live in conditions that border on squalor. If your facility is constantly running out of supplies your parent needs, or if the nursing assistants are told that they need to limit supplies to an unreasonable extent, you should report this activity to the state survey agency that oversees your nursing home.

You Should Know that some facilities have an unwritten policy that forbids the changing of a diaper pad before it is completely wet. Some incontinent pads have special cloth stripes that change color when they are saturated. The color change is visible from the outside of the pad. If only one or two of these colored stripes appears, the pad may not be "wet enough" to change.

Most facilities leave the decision of when to change an incontinent pad up to the nursing assistants, but some facilities monitor and micromanage the use of every item in order to cut costs in every way possible. Some facility managers, who are rewarded for maintaining a low supply budget, warn the nursing assistants that "we are using too many pads, so use them sparingly and do everything you can to conserve." Other facilities may place a restriction on how many items can be used each day.

Some of the unwritten policies that exist in many nursing homes will not be immediately apparent to you but will become recognizable once you sit back, blend in, and quietly observe the staff members in action. Once they get to know you, some of them will open up and share many of their frustrations, meaning they will hand you details about the facility's problems on a silver platter.

A special diet ordered for your parent in accordance with her plan of care has probably been prescribed for her medical benefit, whether it is a low-calorie, no salt, or no sugar diet. Many nurses strictly adhere to an ordered diet, while others turn a blind eye to an occasional deviation from the dietary care plan. A shared philosophy among some nurses is that the benefits of a diet restriction do not always outweigh the consequences when a ninety-year-old diabetic is asking for a small piece of pie.

The same theory is often applied to medications that are intended to serve a beneficial purpose. If the side effects of a daily medication are causing a resident to endure more discomfort than the original ailment, then the purpose may be defeated. For instance, nearly half of the residents at a large nursing home where I worked had a medication order for a liquid stool softener that was intended to make bowel movements more comfortable. Each time the residents were given the medication, even when diluted in juice, they all made the same twisted facial expression that could be interpreted only as severe detestation.

One day, a few of the nurses decided to taste the stool softener to determine whether the medication truly was as distasteful as the residents appeared to attest. (It was ordered in bulk in the form of a community bottle from the nursing home's pharmacy and not billed to a specific resident.) We each took a very small amount, not equal to a full dose. Not only did the medication taste worse than anything I had previously experienced, the taste lingered for an hour or more. These residents were getting it in larger quantities every day! I never gave that medication to another resident without loads of juice and ice cream.

These residents had so many other options, like prune juice, fiber drinks, or a different, better-tasting medication. Hard stools probably would have been more comfortable. I am not going to suggest that you taste each of your parent's medications, but you should weigh the benefits of each treatment against the consequences.

You Should Know whether your parent is receiving routine eyedrops and if he accepts eye medication easily or struggles against the nurse during the procedure. Eyedrops are frequently administered to residents who tightly shut their eyes during the entire process, which can be ordered up to four times per day. I have seen residents become angry and forcibly push away from the eyedrops as they are being administered.

Eyedrops can contain necessary medication or can be for lubrication purposes only. If your parent is receiving eyedrops that are not vital to his health and he resists the procedure, becomes angry, or experiences obvious discomfort each time the drops are administered, you might reconsider having the eyedrops as part of his care plan.

You should be the judge of how well your parent copes with any procedures he or she must partake in. If eyedrops are a problem for your parent but are absolutely necessary, ask the doctor whether they can be given fewer times per day. Alternatively, determine if your parent is able to administer his own drops if the nurse hands him the bottle. Sometimes when residents administer their own eyedrops, they experience less apprehension, but, of course, it is not easy for many residents to do this.

Another consideration for residents who must receive eye medications is that when eyedrops are administered to a resident seated in a chair, it can be very difficult for her to tilt her head back to receive the drops. Many older people cannot lean their heads back to the necessary angle or can do so only with extreme discomfort. If a resident does not have good range of motion in her neck, it might be easier and more comfortable for her to receive eyedrops while in bed. If your parent must receive eyedrops, observe the procedure yourself and determine whether you need to ask the doctor to change the time the drops are delivered to a time when your parent is in bed.

It is the policy at most nursing homes for the nurses to wash their hands and put on gloves before they administer eyedrops to a resident, but this does not always happen. There are too many time constraints, and this important step is skipped quite often. It has been my observation that when one resident gets an eye infection, at least a few other residents also get eye infections, probably a direct result of the lack of hand washing and/or the nurse not wearing gloves during the procedure.

In most nursing homes, a complete skin and body check is done each time a resident is given a bath or shower. Some facilities require the nursing assistants to do this check and then report any bruises, rashes, or open sores to the nurse, who then examines whatever abnormality was reported. Other facilities require the nurse to be called into the shower room to complete the weekly skin check. This was the case at most of the facilities where I worked as a nurse. I was called into the shower room to conduct numerous skin checks only to find that the resident was either already submerged or was half dressed and on his way out of the shower room. Often the nursing assistant calls for the nurse, and the nurse is unable to respond right away. Because the nursing assistants do not have time to wait, residents often miss several of their skin checks.

You Should Know the procedure at your facility for conducting complete skin examinations, especially if your parent is not able to move independently or reposition himself. A pressure sore or open sore that is left undiagnosed and untreated has the potential to cause pain, become infected, and/or lead to amputation. You should know whether your parent is having regular skin checks and ask for the results at every care plan meeting.

You Should Know whether the nursing staff is checking your parent's ears for wax on a regular basis. Excessive earwax buildup can cause dizziness and/or difficulty hearing. It can also be very uncomfortable. Some residents are not able to identify the problem and therefore do not ask to have their ears checked.

Residents who are able to ask for assistance get their ears flushed with a wax-removing liquid. Since residents do not routinely get their ears checked for wax buildup by the facility physician, you should ask the director of nurses to schedule your parent for monthly ear checks by the nurse. Ask for updates at the care plan meetings.

You Should Know if your parent would rather not be bathed by a nursing assistant of the opposite sex. Many female residents are extremely uncomfortable about a bathing arrangement whereby a male nursing assistant performs all of their personal care, but they do not mention their bathing preference until they are asked. You should alert the director of nurses about your parent's preferences.

You Should Know that posting notes in your parent's room is an effective way to remind staff members about your parent's plan of care. Many family members hang a bulletin board in their parent's room and attach large-print messages for staff members, such as "DON'T FORGET DENTIST APPOINTMENT WEDNESDAY," "THICKENED FLUIDS ONLY" or "PLEASE GIVE SNACK BEFORE BED."

You Should Know whether your parent's call bell extends to all points of the room. If your facility has the type of call bell system whereby a cord comes out of the wall, the cord should reach all points in the room where your parent might sit. Many residents find that their call bells are out of reach and they have no way to call for help. In this situation, residents must either yell or wait in their rooms and try to catch the attention of someone walking by in order to get help. You can bring your parent a small, handheld bell to keep on the opposite side of the room in the event she is unable to reach her call bell.

You Should Know the benefits as well as the negative consequences of having your parent's room near the nurse's station. If your parent requires frequent monitoring, a room by the nurse's station will guarantee that more people are looking in on her because that central location is a very busy area with staff members frequently walking past the nearby rooms. Many families request that their parent be close to the nurse's station to be assured of the extra attention, so these rooms have frequent occupancy changes due to the changing needs and requests of residents.

Residents who are at risk for falling are usually given rooms near the nurse's station so the staff can get to them as quickly as possible if their alarms go off. Keep in mind, too, that most business and conversations are conducted in this area, so there is an increased noise level in and around the rooms that are close by. If your parent is semi-independent and enjoys a quiet atmosphere, you should make sure his room is a good distance from the nurse's station. If the opposite is true, ask for a room as close to the station as possible.

You Should Know that keeping a journal of all of the events that occur in the nursing home will help you give a better medical history to a doctor or other professional who needs to know about your parent's course of treatment. Because of turnover in the positions of directors and administrators, you will want to be able to discuss your parent's history with any new management member.

Keep track of important dates and significant occurrences. For instance, if your parent has had room changes, previously ineffective treatments, or any customized arrangement that you asked to be implemented, you want to remember the events as accurately as possible so you can relay the information to a new team of care providers.

THINGS TO BRING YOUR PARENT

The nursing home does not supply your parent with many of the essential items that most residents need. You will need to bring your parent clothes, shoes, a chair for her room, and any electronic devices that she has become accustomed to using. Most facilities provide a bed, a bedside table, and one television set per room.

You Should Know that many facilities do not provide each resident with a television that works via remote control. Many residents must ring their call bell and wait for assistance each time they want the channel changed or the television turned on or off. In addition to a remote control, your parent should have a set of cordless headphones if he shares a room, because his roommate may not wish to be disturbed, or the roommate may have his own television.

You Should Know that you can bring your parent a personal wheelchair so that she will always have one when needed. Many facilities do not have enough wheelchairs for each resident to have one designated as her own, so most of the wheelchairs in the facility are shared by all of the residents. Remember that residents eat while sitting in these chairs and may experience bowel or bladder incontinence. Although the chairs are sometime protected by pads, there are always leaks onto the wheelchairs. The facility wheelchairs are rarely properly sanitized after each contaminating incident and are often visibly dirty with caked-on food.

Most facilities have a policy that requires the staff to clean all the wheelchairs each week. This task is usually delegated to the nursing assistants, who, as you now know, have the heaviest workload of all of the nursing home employees. When shortcuts are taken, this task falls through the cracks, and months can pass before each wheelchair is cleaned.

Another typical problem with wheelchairs in the nursing home is that they are always missing parts. Many times residents are told to "hold up your feet" because the detachable footrests have been removed and misplaced. It is common to see residents being pushed down the hall in a wheelchair while uncomfortably holding up their legs. I have also seen many residents suffer injuries to their feet and ankles because, after holding their legs up for a period of time, they get tired, and when their feet touch the floor, they are quickly brought under the moving chair.

You can bring in a new (or used) wheelchair for your parent, alert the staff that no other residents should use it, and, of course, affix a name label. Once your parent has her own wheelchair, you can personalize it with a seat cushion and a pocketed flap for storing belongings.

You Should Know that if you bring your parent clothing that opens in the front or back, she will be less likely to struggle with staff members to get dressed and undressed each day. Many elderly people have difficulty raising their arms for clothing that must be put on over their heads. Also, because elderly people have such fragile skin, many residents sustain skin tears while having their clothes changed, especially when they are being rushed.

You Should Know that you can decrease your parent's risk of falling by bringing her nonslip footwear and (with permission) applying strips of gripper tape near your parent's bed. It is usually not until after a resident falls that individual safety issues are discussed and implemented. Many residents fall in the nursing home while wearing socks on a linoleum floor, shoes that do not fit properly, or shoes that have no tread.

You Should Know that you can arrange in advance for your parent to order take-out food from local restaurants. You can collect menus from selected restaurants in the area near the nursing home that offer delivery service. Keep the menus in a notebook in your parent's room for the times when he wants a change from or doesn't like what is being served. He can order the food by telephone, you can call it in yourself, or you can ask a staff member to help with the ordering process. You can set up a payment account or leave a small amount of cash with your parent each week.

If you keep a full bowl of candy in your parent's room, staff members will flock to his room more often. It may sound deceptively simple, but I knew a resident who kept a bowl of candy in her room for the staff and as a result enjoyed a constant stream of employee visitors. Her needs were always met because most of the staff members stopped by her room a few times each day to grab a treat.

LEGAL

You Should Know whether your parent's initial admission paperwork includes an arbitration clause that would require you to resolve any disputes between your family and the nursing home with an arbiter rather than in court. The attorneys for many nursing home chains and owners prefer arbitration as a means of dispute resolution because it is less formal, there are fewer evidence rules, and, more important, there are no sympathetic jurors involved.

Arbitration agreements are a convenient way to reduce stress on the court system when both parties agree to this forum in advance. The problem with arbitration agreements in nursing home admission contracts is that the residents are not usually provided the option of whether or not to sign the agreement because their signature is often a requirement of admission to the facility. Many residents do not always know what they are signing or what they are forfeiting when they sign away their rights to be heard in a court of law.

The attorneys who work for the nursing home often choose the arbiter, usually a private judge who might see the nursing home attorneys over and over but will see your family only once.

Regardless of the language used in your parent's admission contract, you should have the contract and all associated paperwork evaluated by an eldercare attorney, if possible, before your parent is admitted.

You Should Know whether your nursing home has any registered sex offenders residing therein. Ask the administrator if she is aware of any offenders living in the facility. Also check with the local police department (who can at least refer you to a local Web site that tracks offenders in your area).

WEB SITES AND SERVICES

You Should Know that you are not alone in your advocacy for better nursing home care. You should visit the Web sites below to learn about other efforts toward nursing home reform:

- National Citizens' Coalition for Nursing Home Reform (NCCNHR) is an advocacy group that promotes better nursing home care and offers information about recent developments in the law regarding nursing home care. The groups' Web site is www.nccnhr.com.

- The site http://elderly-abuse.com offers current news and information about nursing home abuse and progress toward making changes in long-term care.
- The site http://www.cms.hhs.gov lists the nation's SFF (Special Focus Facility) nursing homes, which are the facilities with the poorest inspection results nationwide. Type "special focus facilities" in the search box.
- The site http://www.familiesforbettercare.org lists independent nursing home advocates in each state.

You Should Know that massage therapists provide services to nursing home residents in most communities. There are many benefits to therapeutic massage, including pain relief, improved circulation, and reduced stress. The social worker in your facility should be able to recommend a local massage therapist.

Finally, know that if you are kind and amicable when dealing with the nursing home staff, you will reap greater benefits for your parent. I have seen many family members make unreasonable demands on the nursing staff in a disrespectful and condescending tone every time they visited the facility. Their actions did not motivate staff members to provide additional help to the parent of that family.

I worked in one facility where a family member was so rude and demanding that the nursing staff actually turned and walked the opposite direction when they saw her coming down the hall. Rather than conversing with her, the staff shunned her each time she entered the building. It is difficult to be a good advocate for your parent when the staff does not want to communicate with you.

CHAPTER 7

NURSING HOME
TRAGEDIES

This chapter consists of news stories I found while researching nursing homes in newspapers from nearly every state. I have included a brief description to help you understand some of the dangers that exist in our country's nursing homes. Unfortunately, many of these stories are disturbing and difficult to read. My intention here is not to scare you but rather to shed additional light on these very significant tragedies and possibly help you to prevent an accident of a similar nature. If you are interested in reading the entire version of any of these articles, the publication information is printed in the notes section at the end of the book.

ABUSE AND NEGLECT

Arkansas

The *Times-Picayune*[1] reported that the Little Rock county coroner exhumed the bodies of six former nursing home residents in five years. "All of the cases had been reported as natural deaths. But when Malcolm and his team finished their work, they determined that the actual cause of death in each case was neglect." Two of the deaths were found to be from medication errors and four from suffocation. One of the residents had been found "wedged between his mattress and the side rails of his bed, wearing a restraint." The article states that Marc Malcolm helped pass a state law that now requires nursing homes to notify the coroner whenever a nursing home resident dies.

California

The *Santa Barbara News Press*[2] reported that a nurse killed herself because no one would listen to her complaints about poor care at the nursing home where she worked. She left a journal that prompted state prosecutors to investigate the Santa Barbara nursing home. The nursing home "pleaded no contest to two felony counts of elder abuse." One resident suffered from malnutrition, body tremors, and open wounds with maggot infestations. The other resident died from an infection due to an incorrectly placed feeding tube in his stomach.

The article also describes a criminal felony conviction against another nursing home involving the deaths of two nursing home residents who suffered from heat-related illnesses after a heat wave. Six other residents suffered from heatstroke or heat exhaustion. "The nursing home did not have air conditioning."

The *Press Enterprise*[3] reported that a nursing home administrator "has been criminally charged for allegedly failing to report an assault that took place against a patient." The assault took place against a patient who was allegedly choked during an altercation with a nursing assistant. The nursing assistant later pleaded guilty to elder abuse. Administrators are required by law to report suspected abuse to the state agency that oversees nursing homes.

Colorado

The *Denver Post*,[4] citing a former nursing home employee, reported that a "nursing home didn't do everything possible to revive a patient, then destroyed part of the patient's paperwork." The autopsy showed that the resident, who "choked to death on her own vomit," may have survived had basic lifesaving procedures been performed. The nurse's aide reports that she saw a nurse walk away from the resident without trying to clear her airway and say, "I don't want to deal with vomit." The aide then apparently watched the nurse remove the advance directive from the medical chart, destroy it, get a blank document, and insert that in the medical chart. According to the nurse's aide, the document indicated that the resident wanted to be resuscitated.

The same nursing home had been cited "for shortcomings by state inspectors 18 times" the previous year. In the past three years, the facility has been cited for "either hiring employees with records of abuse or failing to properly report and investigate reports of abuse, neglect or maltreatment." The facility also has "one of the lowest nurse-to-patient ratios" in the county.

Connecticut

The *Hartford Courant*[5] reported that an eighty-two-year-old nursing home resident was choked to death by the chair's belt when she slipped down in her chair. A state ombudsman said that she "and ombudsmen in regional offices around the state have noticed an increase in restraint use."

Delaware

The *News Journal*[6] reported the death of a resident being investigated at an area nursing home. The resident died after being found "accidentally hanged by the seat belt on his wheelchair." The investigative report showed that "the victim's arms were above his head, with his T-shirt bunched up around his neck and the seat belt was around his neck holding him up." The medical examiner determined that he died of asphyxia.

Florida

The *Miami Herald*[7] reported that a seventy-three-year-old bedridden nursing home resident died after being bitten by hundreds of fire ants. The resident was admitted to the nursing home to recuperate from surgery. He died "of shock from the amount of ant poison in his body, the medical examiner's report said." The article stated that "his back, arms, chest, neck, head and shoulders were covered in ant bites." The facility was being sprayed by a pest control company every week.

Georgia

The *Atlanta Journal-Constitution*[8] reported that state inspectors have penalized a nursing home for allowing a resident's ear to become infested with maggots. Inspectors had cited the home for poor conditions the previous year. The article also noted that resident advocates "concluded the state issued the appropriate citation in just two of seventy legitimate abuse and neglect cases." The state ombudsman's office said, "Inspectors should have investigated more thoroughly on their earlier visit to determine what caused the infestation."

The article reported that a "resident told an inspector that family members on at least one visit spent most of their time killing flies." The facility was threatened with closure in 2001, but inspectors were satisfied with improvements.

Idaho

The *Times-News*[9] reported that an Idaho nursing home had its license revoked due to an inspection that found some residents to be in immediate danger. The inspection also revealed the "facility's failure to properly monitor, care for and keep accurate clinical records." The facility administrator "has 28 days to file an appeal with the state." If no appeal is received, the facility must close.

Indiana

The *Indianapolis Star*[10] reported that a nursing home resident died after staff failed to perform resuscitation or call 911 when the resident was found with no pulse. The resident had indicated in writing that he wanted to be resuscitated in the event his heart stopped. According to the article, facility was sanctioned and "will not be able to admit new patients for 30 days."

Iowa

The *Des Moines Register*[11] reported that a nursing home was fined $5,300 after one of its residents died of kidney failure. The resident died at the hospital due to " kidney failure, poor food intake and weight loss." The article reported, "Earlier that day, the staff at the home wrote in the resident's file that there were no signs and symptoms of dehydration." According to state inspectors, the facility did not "provide sufficient fluids and identify and respond to the resident's recent weight loss."

The same article reported that several other area facilities were fined $100 to $200 for "allegedly failing to conduct required background checks on employees."

Kentucky

The *Lexington Herald Leader*[12] reported that an investigation at a Kentucky nursing home found that "40 percent of the residents received more than nine medications and that some got up to 25—mostly without clinical justification and with little regard for how the drugs might interact." Investigators found that "one out of six patients, an unusually high proportion, had feeding tubes. Many were unnecessary; one woman with a feeding tube offered investigators a candy bar—and proceeded to eat one herself. The tubes, investigators decided, often appeared to be inserted for the convenience of the staff." They also found residents "sedated with powerful psychotropics that the medical community says are ill-advised for the elderly."

Louisiana

The *Shreveport Times*[13] reported that a nursing home resident died after a "licensed practical nurse at the facility inserted a Foley catheter into the ninety-seven-year-old man without a physician's consent and without documenting the procedure in the patient's medical chart." The resident bled profusely from his penis after the procedure, which may have been performed incorrectly, but he was not transferred to the hospital until the next day.

Maine

The *Portland Press Herald*[14] reported that conditions at a Portland nursing home are being investigated by the state after a resident was dropped by a nurse's aide and broke both her legs. The resident, whose care plan called for the assistance of two nurse's aides and a mechanical lift for transfers, was being transferred by only one nurse's aide. The resident later died. A subsequent investigation at the facility found "improper use of physical restraints; public discussion of a patient's physical condition; improper care of bedsores and failure to ensure regular doctor's visits."

Massachusetts

The *Cape Cod Times*[15] reported that a nurse's aide was sentenced to eight months in jail for "abusing two elderly nursing home patients." He was found guilty of tripping and taunting one resident and flicking the hearing aid of another resident. The assistant attorney general said, "What troubled me more with each of these incidents is that they were followed by a laugh" from the nurse's aide. He will not be able to work in any long-term-care facility in the state of Massachusetts.

Michigan

The *Detroit Free Press*[16] reported that a Detroit nursing home had its license revoked after an annual inspection that resulted in forty-five health citations (the national average is seven to nine violations). The inspection report showed that residents had bedsores and were also "wet from urinating on themselves" and were "sleeping in beds with no linens." In addition, "prescribed diets were not followed," "medications were not stored properly or were not available," and "required staff levels were not maintained."

Minnesota

The *Star Tribune*[17] reported that two nursing homes were cited for neglect. One nursing home resident was not given her Coumadin, a blood-thinning medication, for seven days. According to the article, another resident, who had a weakened immune system due to chemotherapy, "died of infection and pneumonia two weeks after he was placed with a roommate who had a drug-resistant staph infection with open sores on his legs." Family members said that they complained about finding bloody bandages on the sink and were told there was no danger. The home was fined $8,000.

Montana

The *Great Falls Tribune*[18] reported that a seventy-year-old nursing home resident "caught on fire while smoking a cigarette" at the nursing home where he lived. He suffered burns over 80 percent of his body and died the next day. According to the article, the nursing home staff had, on other occasions, extinguished his smoldering clothing. A state report found that the nursing home "failed to give each resident adequate supervision and assistance to prevent accidents." A Department of Public Health and Human Services investigator said, "The home's smoking room also lacked a metal, self-closing container, a violation of its own policy."

Nevada

A Nevada nursing home that was previously investigated for patient abuse after six residents died in one day (four possibly from the flu) and for Medicaid fraud was placed on the Special Focus Facility list with the Centers for Medicare and Medicaid Services. The agency now lists the Special Focus Facilities that are the nation's poorest performers.[19]

New Mexico

The *AARP Bulletin*[20] reported a story about an undercover state agent who posed as an Alzheimer's resident to discover the quality of care delivered in a particular nursing home. He took notes and passed them to his "visitors," who were also state employees. He lost ten pounds during his five-day stay because he could not eat the food, but the nursing home records indicated he ate 50 percent of each meal. He witnessed nursing assistants eating off the residents' plates. According to the article, he watched residents struggle to no avail to open their packages of crackers and nobody helped them. He later saw the staff gather the unopened crackers and eat them.

He reportedly did not see any abuse but saw "chilling indifference to the residents and a troubling lack of care." He was not bathed and did not change his clothes the entire time he was there. He also said that he was not offered any type of liquid other than with meals.

Although on a locked unit, he reported staffing shortages as the reason the door to the unit remained propped open, thus allowing the nurse to watch over two units. The undercover resident stated that he wandered off the unit, and no one ever stopped or questioned him.

North Carolina

The *Charlotte Observer*[21] reported that injuries, even fatal injuries, are not being reported to the state because "when nursing home officials know how the injuries occurred and don't suspect abuse, neglect or mistreatment" there is no requirement to report the incident. The article detailed a death that occurred when an eighty-nine-year-old resident fell five feet from a mechanical lift used to transfer her from her bed to a wheelchair. The incident "was not reported to or investigated by the state" since abuse was not suspected.

Pennsylvania

The *Tribune-Review*[22] reported that a licensed practical nurse pleaded guilty to charges that she allegedly struck four nursing home residents who resisted taking their medications. Citing court documents, the newspaper reported that several of her co-workers told investigators that they witnessed her being abusive. She allegedly "grabbed one woman by the hair roughly and tried to force her mouth open" and then "held the woman's nose shut to force her to open her mouth."

Another co-worker stated that she witnessed the nurse "smack a patient across the face, causing her lip to bleed." A resident who made a mess out of her diaper was allegedly smacked in the hip. Another co-worker said that he believed while the nurse struggled with a patient, she "gave the patient a black eye."

The *Times-Tribune*[23] reported that the death of an Alzheimer's patient was being investigated because if the doctor had "examined her as he claimed, he could not have missed a malignant tumor in her right breast that caused a deformity and a 2.5 centimeter oozing sore." The sixty-nine-year-old patient died because the cancer spread to her lungs, liver, and bones. The facility staff eventually sent her to the hospital where hospital workers "noted her extremely poor hygiene," and her records showed that she "had been bathed only six times in eight and a half months.

Texas

A man in Texas reported that his mother died after spending one month in a local nursing home, and he cannot get anyone to take action.[24] He reports that she "walked, talked, could eat on her own" before she went into the facility, but that "she left out of there an invalid." He said that when he asked the facility to transport his mother to the hospital after he reported that she could be having a heart attack, the staff refused, so he called the state. He quotes the hospital doctor as saying that his mother "had not been fed, given any water, and that she had abusive bruising." Her death certificate lists malnutrition. "I want them to face the same consequences that I would have faced if I had taken my mother to the hospital in that condition."

Utah

The *Daily Herald*[25] reported that a Provo nursing home was cited for putting its residents in immediate jeopardy. The citation was issued after a resident told the nursing staff she was going to hoard her medication and use it to kill herself. After the resident killed herself with an overdose, the state conducted an investigation that revealed that the resident's threat went undocumented, the resident's mental status was not assessed, and the nursing home did not investigate the death.

Virginia

The *Richmond Times-Dispatch*[26] reported that the death of a seventy-nine-year-old woman at a nursing home is being investigated. She died after sliding out of her wheelchair and was found hanging by the wheelchair's seatbelt. The resident was apparently left unattended. The autopsy report indicated that the resident died of asphyxia.

Washington

The *Seattle Times*[27] reported that "[s]tate regulators have taken the rare step of deciding to close a Spokane nursing home, saying residents are in imminent danger." Investigators found over thirty violations and in examining three deaths "found fault with the home's care in two of those deaths." According to the article, "the state repeatedly fined the home and reports allege the staff failed to give medications, neglected wounds and shoved elderly patients." Three administrators resigned after learning the home had no liability insurance.

West Virginia

The *Charleston Gazette*[28] reported that "[s]ome nursing home residents at a state-owned facility were unsupervised, abused and not given proper medical attention, according to federal review." The newspaper stated, citing the federal report, "the facility failed to protect a resident from possible abuse by the nursing staff."

According to the article, a resident was "abruptly taken by the elbow and put back in her room" after refusing the nurse's order to "Get to your room!" The article notes that the report identified other problems such as "Nurses failed to follow a doctor's order to provide continuous oxygen for a resident. A resident's blood pressure was checked only once a month, even though it was meant to be taken once a week. A call light for a resident who had to go to the bathroom was inaccessible, and fire walls and doors were not up to standards."

The article describes a man who died after "allegedly being given a 4,000 cc enema" and a resident who was given another resident's blood-thinning medication and "bled to death."

AMPUTATIONS

Mississippi

The *Clarion-Ledger*[29] reported that a nursing home resident had to have her leg amputated after she developed bedsores. An attorney for the family indicated that the staff did not reposition her in bed, and she often lied in her own waste. According to the attorney, "most of the abuse occurred when the facility was short staffed."

Nebraska

The *Journal Star*[30] reported that an "Omaha nursing home is accused of providing poor care that led to the amputation of an elderly woman's legs and then allowing her to fall out of a wheelchair after the operations." The resident had developed gangrene in her right leg, which required amputation, then developed an ulcer on her left foot, which went untreated, became infected, and was subsequently amputated. After the surgeries, she was a passenger in a facility van but not properly strapped in her wheelchair when she fell out of the chair and injured her head. The article reported that the resident has since moved to another facility.

BEDSORES

Connecticut

The *Hartford Courant*[31] reported that the former owner of a nursing home "will be charged with manslaughter" for alleged neglect of a resident that led to his death. "An autopsy by the state's medical examiner's office found that a resident died of sepsis," according to the article. The family claimed that the septic shock was due to infected bedsores and malnutrition. The family also claims that the facility "did not have enough nurses to care for patients." The health department had noted several patient-care violations over a two-year period.

DOCUMENT FALSIFICATION

Hawaii

The *Honolulu Advertiser*[32] reported that the Medicaid Investigations Division discovered "questionable practices," including "falsification of records and kickback schemes for medication at a long-term-care center." According to the deputy attorney general, "some nurses were told to leave gaps in resident reports so they could later insert whatever was needed to justify billing for a service."

Iowa

The *Des Moines Register*[33] reported that a nursing home executive "has been indicted by a federal grand jury for allegedly ordering caregivers to conceal a resident's injuries from health inspectors." A resident was injured and hospitalized after she fell out of a chair. According to prosecutors, a month before the injury, the home was cited for failing to adequately supervise and protect residents from injury. The nurse consultant who was helping the facility prepare for the state inspection allegedly agreed to conceal information, while another nurse allegedly gave a list of injured residents, which omitted the hospitalized resident, to the inspectors.

According to the article, the federal government began requiring states to report the total number of complaints received, but Rhode Island is one of the states that has not yet reported. "Most information about complaints stays secret."

FALLS

Arizona

The *Arizona Republic*[34] reported that "a year after state health officials uncovered serious violations at a state-run nursing home for veterans, a new report revealed that poor care since then has led to injuries among several residents." The article reported that one resident was found with a wound bandage that "hadn't been changed in two days. When it was removed, they found that the wound had gotten much worse." Another resident "fell 18 times from June 25 to October 31. Another resident fell nine times." The article noted that the inspection was "prompted by two complaints from the public and reports of several incidents from the home."

Rhode Island

The *Providence Journal*[35] reported that a Rhode Island nursing home was ordered to "immediately correct the inadequate staffing that led to repeated falls by a patient." A resident who fell eleven times was considered to be in immediate jeopardy. "Although her care plan called for supervision when she walked, three of her falls were not even witnessed and the nursing home took no action to prevent future falls." The inspection also revealed that "[f]our other residents were found to have fallen multiple times because they lacked supervision. One suffered a fractured hip."

FIRES/FIRE SAFETY VIOLATIONS

Connecticut

The *Hartford Courant*[36] reported that top executives who ran the nursing home where a fire killed sixteen people "could face criminal charges" for "failing to properly protect the elderly and infirm patients who were victimized." The article reported that the "probe is looking into whether companies were criminally negligent in failing to properly screen incoming patients to see if their backgrounds and conditions might endanger other patients." The fire was started by a resident with a mental illness and a history of substance abuse.

Massachusetts

The *Boston Globe*[37] reported that a "grand jury is investigating the death of a nursing home resident who suffered a brain injury after falling down a flight of stairs." The dementia resident allegedly went through a door that should have been locked, which led to the stairs. "State and police reports suggest the door was not working properly that night." The previous year, according to the article, the Public Health Department had temporarily suspended admissions to the facility while it reviewed the home's safety precautions and staffing.

Tennessee

The *Tennessean*[38] reported that a building code expert who examined a Nashville nursing home the day after a fire claimed sixteen lives said he told his supervisors at the Department of Health that he found building code violations. He also said that the state did not properly investigate the fire and that the nursing home had not been cited. The nursing home had been inspected by the state three months prior to the fire and was found to be in compliance with state and federal building regulations.

Wyoming

The *Casper Star Tribune*[39] reported that "Wyoming has the fourth highest percentage of nursing homes with fire safety deficiencies in the nation, according to a government report." The newspaper reported that the Government Accountability Office concluded 94.9 percent of the thirty-nine nursing homes in Wyoming had fire safety deficiencies based on information as of December 2003. Also included in the article, "Nationally, 58.9 percent of 16,334 surveyed nursing homes had fire safety deficiencies."

FORCED FEEDINGS

Maryland

The *Baltimore Sun*[40] reported that an eighty-nine-year-old nursing home resident was fed to death after nursing home staff left a feeding tube running continuously until her "abdomen was markedly protuberant and she was short of breath and moaning." An investigation showed that "more than eight times the amount of liquid than had been prescribed by her doctor" had been delivered to her eighty-nine-pound body and that the feeding was not supposed to begin until the following day. According to the article, state officials fined the nursing home a $20,000 penalty, which also included other violations.

South Dakota

The *Argus Leader*[41] reported that the children of an eighty-seven-year-old nursing home patient who was suffocated want the former nurse's aide prosecuted. The nurse's aide is accused of forcing food into the elderly man's mouth until he suffocated to death.

Wisconsin

The *Journal Sentinel*[42] reported that a seventy-nine-year-old woman died after she experienced an episode of low blood sugar, which required an immediate glucagon (sugar) injection, but instead was force-fed Jello and juice. The paper reported that the licensed practical nurse allegedly pinched the resident's nose to "try to force her to ingest the food, refused to call for help and may have given a sugar lowering insulin shot." The resident had a swallowing problem and died within an hour of the event. According to the article, the nurse was sentenced to "13 months behind bars and 35 months of probation."

HEAT-RELATED DEATHS

Michigan

The *Detroit Free Press*[43] reported that a state senator planned to introduce a bill that would require all nursing homes in Michigan to have air conditioners in residents' rooms. This proposal came after three nursing home residents died and five others were hospitalized due to heat-related illnesses.

Missouri

The *St. Louis Today*[44] reported that four nursing home residents "died within 48 hours of each other after temperatures exceeded 95 degrees" at the nursing home. The deaths were ruled by the medical examiner to be from hyperthermia. The article reported that the families of the victims allege that the nursing home managers knew about the dangerous conditions but "failed to replace what they knew was an inadequate air-conditioning system, even after employees complained."

Texas

The *Houston Chronicle*[45] reported that a Waco nursing home resident was left in a van for several hours and died of hyperthermia. The van driver picked up the eighty-seven-year-old resident after her doctor's appointment, drove her back to the nursing home, then left the facility in another vehicle. It was 97 degrees outside. She was found approximately four hours later, in her wheelchair, in the back of the van. The van driver was arrested and charged with criminally negligent homicide.

INADEQUATE STAFFING

Delaware

The *News Journal*[46] reported that "three days of fact-finding hearings on the system of care for Delaware's nursing home patients has revealed that nursing facilities violating the state's staffing requirements are not being penalized." The head of the state's Division of Long-Term-Care Resident Protection said that "11 nursing homes were cited in 2001 and 2002 for falling below the state's minimum staffing requirements" and that "no action was taken because she did not think the citation would be upheld through the appeal process."

Louisiana

The *Daily Advertiser*[47] reported that "more oversight is needed of the agencies that provide temporary nurses to medical facilities." The article noted, "Staffing nursing homes with dependable nurses and nurses' aides is a nationwide problem. Some are incompetent or uncaring. Some are dangerous." All agencies that provide temporary staffing do not do drug testing or criminal background checks on their employees because the "Louisiana Department of Health and Hospitals does not provide monitoring and oversight of agencies that provide temporary staff for nursing facilities."

A study conducted by the House Government Reform Committee revealed nationwide abuse in nursing homes. "The report documented instances of residents being punched, slapped, choked, or kicked by staff members or other residents . . . instances of abuse appear to be on the rise."

Missouri

The *Kansas City Star*[48] found, after an investigation into the state's nursing homes, that nursing homes in Missouri with less than average staffing had more resident injuries than those that had at least average staffing. The article chronicled several residents. One resident complained of foot pain for three weeks, until his wife finally insisted he be taken to the hospital. His leg had gangrene and had to be amputated. Another resident was found on the floor without a pulse, but the nurse thought that he was one of the residents who was not to be resuscitated and did not perform CPR or call 911. His son was unaware of the circumstances surrounding his death until he was told by a reporter.

The article points out that nurse's aides in Missouri are required to have seventy-five hours of training and one hundred hours of on-the-job supervision, whereas manicurists need four hundred hours of training.

Another resident nearly died after being connected to a feeding tube and receiving more than double the correct amount. "The liquid food was going in so fast that it came out of the resident's mouth. The resident stopped breathing and was rushed to a hospital." The nurse apparently stated that the nursing duties were too heavy, and included being responsible for residents on two floors. According to the article, the nurse was fired.

SEXUAL ASSAULT

Alabama

The *Montgomery Advertiser*[49] reported that a ninety-year-old nursing home resident with dementia was raped and that the facility has been cited for hiring two nurses with histories of abuse. According to the district attorney, "the evidence collected was semen." One nurse admitted on his employment application that, "while working at a local nursing home, I was accused of sexually abusing an 86-year-old. I was indicted by the grand jury. . . . My case was dismissed for lacking evidence." The district attorney said, "Fortunately for us in this case, we do have physical evidence."

Illinois

A nursing home in Illinois was reportedly aware of repeated sexual assaults against an eighty-two-year-old female nursing home resident, yet did nothing to stop the resident's former landlord from visiting her in the nursing home. The abuser pleaded guilty to criminal sexual abuse.[50]

New Jersey

The *Star-Ledger*[51] reported that a forty-one-year-old male recreational worker at a nursing home was charged with aggravated sexual assault on a mentally incapacitated eighty-four-year-old female resident.

Ohio

The *Cincinnati Enquirer*[52] reported that according to a senior rights group, Ohio ranks third in the nation with convicted sex offenders living in nursing homes. The group compared sex-offender registries in thirty-seven states against a list of nursing home addresses and reported that 380 rapists, child molesters, and other convicted sex offenders live in 298 nursing homes nationwide. The list includes thirty-nine sex offenders in Ohio. The article noted, "Unlike homeowners who get postcards sent by county sheriffs to inform them of registered sex offenders in their neighborhood, such cards typically do not reach residents of nursing homes." The article points out that readers can view the national study about sex offenders in nursing homes at http://www.APerfectCause.org.

Oregon

The *Albany Democrat Herald*[53] reported that a male nursing home worker was convicted of raping and assaulting Alzheimer's residents that were in his care. He worked the night shift, sometimes alone. He helped patients bathe and dress and allegedly admitted to a co-worker that he "was sexually attracted to elderly women." He was found guilty of twenty-four counts, "one count of first-degree rape, two counts of first-degree sodomy, five of first-degree unlawful sexual penetration, eleven of first-degree sexual assault, two of third-degree sexual assault and one of private indecency."

Vermont

The *Burlington Free Press*[54] reported that a nursing home nurse was charged with sexual abuse of a nursing home resident. The newspaper, citing court documents, stated that the nurse and her co-worker allegedly participated in sexual activity in the resident's bed while the resident was in the bed. She also assisted her male co-worker "in an attempt to have nonconsensual sex with the resident." According to the article, the resident was unable to speak.

THEFT

Kansas

The *Lawrence Journal*[55] reported that a woman who was on probation for cocaine possession was hired at a nursing home to work as a nurse's aide. She "eventually began squeezing morphine gel out of patients' skin patches and giving it to herself." A resident advocate stated that the current list of offenses that would preclude nursing home employment includes "sex crimes, violent felonies, and mistreatment of a dependent adult but does not include drug-related crimes." This particular facility did not have drug screening policies for prospective employees. According to the article, the director of nurses and the administrator of the facility have since left.

Oklahoma

The *Tulsa World*[56] reported that the Medicaid Fraud Control Unit of Oklahoma investigated a nursing home administrator accused of taking $3,100 from resident trust accounts. She pleaded guilty to one felony count. One of her probation conditions is that she not be employed by any facility that accepts Medicaid payments. The administrator was also a former investigator for the state of Oklahoma.

WANDERING INCIDENTS

Delaware

The *News Journal*[57] reported that an Alzheimer's resident wandered into a walk-in freezer in the facility's kitchen department. Employees had been watching a sporting event on television when she entered the freezer. She was found "five hours after she went missing." The resident died a month later from complications of severe frostbite. The article reported that the facility has since installed a security system and locks on the kitchen doors.

New Hampshire

The *Union Leader*[58] reported that a nursing home resident, who knew how to open the lock, exited the nursing home's locked door and was found outside, unconscious, in below-freezing temperature. She died from hypothermia. The article also mentioned that in January 2003, an Alzheimer's resident at another nursing home in New Hampshire was found dead outside the facility, covered in snow and wearing only a T-shirt and pants.

New York

The *New York Times*[59] reported that a missing nursing home resident with Alzheimer's disease, who was later found in a puddle of water on the roof of a Queens nursing home, later died of exposure. The incident occurred during the month of February. Her son stated that "on her best day she could not have gone up those stairs alone." According to the article, the police are investigating the death.

CHAPTER 8

IMPORTANT INFORMATION

Use the following checklist to identify any issues that you and your parent find unacceptable. If a listed item is acceptable, mark it as such in the appropriate column. If the issue needs further attention, place a checkmark in the column that reminds you to speak with either the administrator or the director of nurses. If you need to bring something to the attention of other family members, mark that column to remind yourself to raise the issue at the next Family Council meeting.

NURSING HOME CHECKLIST			
ISSUE	ACCEPTABLE	DIRECTOR ADMINISTRATOR	FAMILY COUNCIL
Are Alzheimer's residents on locked or alarmed unit?			
Is the staff-to-resident ratio adequate?			
Is there a supervisor on duty on weekends?			
Is there a no-overtime policy for nurses and nursing assistants?			
Are sixteen-hour shifts permitted?			
What time is my parent getting up to start the day?			
Is my parent fed his/her entire meal?			

NURSING HOME CHECKLIST			
ISSUE	ACCEPTABLE	DIRECTOR ADMINISTRATOR	FAMILY COUNCIL
Does the staff reposition my parent frequently enough?			
Is my parent taken to the dining room in nightclothes?			
How many baths does my parent get a week?			
Do I need to get a doctor's order for an over-the-counter medicine to be kept in the room?			
Does my facility use agency staff every day or occasionally?			
Does my facility use MNAs to cover my parent's unit instead of a nurse?			
What plan of care was devised at the last care plan meeting?			
Does my parent have any complaints that I need to bring to the attention of the managers?			
Does my parent have the physician of his/her choosing?			
Does my parent understand the purpose of each of his/her medications?			
Does my parent have access to a private area to visit with family and friends?			
Are there staff members with whom my parent does not get along?			
Does my parent have access to a telephone?			

NURSING HOME CHECKLIST			
ISSUE	**ACCEPTABLE**	**DIRECTOR ADMINISTRATOR**	**FAMILY COUNCIL**
Is my parent able to self-administer his/ her medications?			
Does the facility readily deliver copies of records that I request?			
Are my parent's monthly blood draws (if any) being done?			
Is the staffing information posted?			
Is a nurse who is familiar with my parent completing his/her assessments?			
Do my parent's dentures fit properly?			
Does my parent have a catheter when he/she could go to the bathroom if given the necessary assistance?			
Does my parent have a bracelet for personal identification?			
Is my parent involved in activities that are of interest to him/her?			
Does my parent need special eating utensils?			
Are healthful, substantial snacks available?			
Does the facility conduct background checks?			
Does the facility have an air conditioner?			
Is the building equipped with an alarm to prevent confused residents from exiting?			
Is a suitable alternative meal available when my parent does not want what is served?			

NURSING HOME CHECKLIST			
ISSUE	ACCEPTABLE	DIRECTOR ADMINISTRATOR	FAMILY COUNCIL
Are staff members who are visibly sick taking care of my parent?			
Is my parent's roommate well suited for him/her?			
Is my parent taking any medications that are intended to subdue his/her behavior?			
Is a copy of my parent's advance directives in the front of his/her chart?			
Does my parent have access to a dentist, eye doctor, and podiatrist?			
Does the facility offer my parent a flu shot each winter?			
Is there a water pitcher in my parent's room?			
Do the kitchen personnel help my parent fill out the weekly menu?			
Are prisoners working in the facility?			
Is my parent capable of keeping his/her own hearing aid in his/her room?			
Does my parent's bed work properly?			
Does my parent's call bell reach all parts of the room?			
Is the call bell answered in a timely fashion?			
With how many people does my parent share a bathroom?			
Does the facility have sufficient supplies?			
How does my parent cope with eyedrops?			

NURSING HOME CHECKLIST			
ISSUE	**ACCEPTABLE**	**DIRECTOR ADMINISTRATOR**	**FAMILY COUNCIL**
Is the facility doing complete skin checks?			
Is the facility doing ear examinations?			
Is my parent bathed by a same-sex nursing assistant?			
Does the facility have a pet that my parent is allergic to/does not like?			

MEDICAL PERSONNEL

TITLE	NAME	TELEPHONE
Administrator		
Medical Director		
Physician/Physician's Asst.		
Nurse Practitioner		
Director of Nurses		
Asst. Director of Nurses		
Infection Control Nurse		
Unit Manager		
Staff Medication Nurse		
Staff Treatment Nurse		
Medication Nursing Asst.		
Nursing Assistant		
Nursing Assistant		
Feeding Assistant		

NONMEDICAL PERSONNEL

TITLE	NAME	TELEPHONE
Director of Social Services		
Social Worker		
Activities Director		
Activities Assistant		
Director of Food Services		
Chef/Kitchen Employee		
Director of Housekeeping		
Housekeeper/Laundry		
Director of Maintenance		
Maintenance Worker		
Seamstress		
Beautician		

STAFF NAMES AND NUMBERS

TITLE	NAME	TELEPHONE
Dietitian		
Podiatrist		
Dentist		
Ophthalmologist		
Wound Specialist		
Speech Therapist		
Occupational Therapist		
Physical Therapist		
Pharmacist		
Massage Therapist		

STATE LICENSING/MONITORING AGENCIES

AGENCY	TELEPHONE
State Ombudsman's Office	
State Survey Agency	
State Board of Nursing	
Licensure Agency for Nursing Assistants	

WOUND CARE CHECKLIST

PROCEDURE	YES	NO
Is the doctor aware of my parent's wound?		
Have pictures been taken in order to mark the progression of the wound healing or worsening?		
Is the staff repositioning my parent at least every two hours and keeping pressure off the wound?		
Has the doctor written a treatment order to change the dressing every day?		
Has the wound specialist been consulted?		
Has the dietitian been consulted?		
Are frequent nurse's notes kept regarding the status of the wound?		
Would this wound be helped by a special mattress?		

Use the following checklist if your parent has a fall or an injury while at the nursing home. List the type of accident, the type of injury, the proposed action that the director of nurses believes will prevent the incident from recurring, whether the doctor has been notified, and the date of the event.

INJURY CHECKLIST

TYPE OF ACCIDENT	INJURY	CORRECTIVE ACTION	MD	DATE

MEDICATION CHART

MEDICATION	DOSE	PURPOSE	START DATE	STOP DATE

FAMILY COUNCIL MEMBERS

MEMBER NAME	TELEPHONE

CONCLUSION

Thank you for allowing me to present to you my suggestions and opinions regarding nursing homes and the care that residents receive therein. I had two goals in mind when I put this book together. First, I hoped to be able to enlighten anyone who is not familiar with the way most nursing homes operate and routinely deliver substandard care. My second goal was to help as many elderly residents as possible to get better nursing home care. It is my sincere hope that I achieved those objectives.

If you have any questions regarding the material in this book, you can reach me via e-mail at longtermcarelaw@aol.com. If I cannot personally answer your question, I will refer you to someone who can. Good luck with your mission to get better nursing home care.

NOTES

1. Jeffrey Meitrodt, "Arkansas Turnaround," *Times-Picayune*, April 21, 2005.

2. "Suicide Note Opened Window into Elder Abuse," *Santa Barbara News-Press*, August 4, 2002.

3. Jose Arballo Jr., "Care Official Goes on Trial," *Press Enterprise*, April 10, 2002.

4. Marcos Mocine-McQueen, "Facility Did Little to Revive Patient Nurse's Aide Says Records Destroyed," *Denver Post*, April 13, 2003.

5. Garret Condon, "Death Stirs Action on Nursing Home Restraints," *Hartford Courant*, May 13, 2002.

6. Terri Sanginiti, "Second Patient's Death Investigated," *News Journal*, February 8, 2003.

7. "$1.9M Settlement Reached in Nursing Home Death," *Miami Herald*, March 12, 2005."

8. Carrie Teegardin, "After Prodding, State Agency Cites Jonesboro Nursing Home," *Atlanta Journal-Constitution*, November 19, 2002.

9. Nate Poppino, "State to Revoke Gooding Nursing Home's License," *Times-News*, December 8, 2007.

10. Diana Penner, "Sanctions Tied to Patient's Death," *Indianapolis Star*, February 4, 2005.

11. Kauffman Clark, "Sioux City Care Site Fined in Resident's Death," *Des Moines Register*, April 13, 2005.

12. Louise Taylor and Lee Mueller, "Laxity at Breathitt Nursing Home," *Lexington Herald Leader*, February 29, 2004.

13. Loresha Wilson, "Nurse Due in Court over Death of Patient," *Shreveport Times*, September 2, 2004.

14. Kelley Bouchard, "Nursing Home Focus of Inquiry," *Portland Press Herald*, March 25, 2004.

15. Robin Lord, "Judge Orders Jail Time for Abusive Aide," *Cape Cod Times*, April 9, 2005.

16. Cecil Angel, "Safety Concerns Trigger Closure of Nursing Home," *Detroit Free Press*, August 7, 2003.

17. Donna Halvorsen, "2 Nursing Homes Cited for Patient Neglect," *Star Tribune*, October 29, 2004.

18. Karen Ogden Ivanova, "State Warns Browning Nursing Home after Patient Burns to Death," *Great Falls Tribune*, April 19, 2002.

19. Auburn Hutton, "Carson City Nursing Home Named One of Nation's Worst," KOLO TV, November 29, 2007, http://elderly-abuse.com.

20. Barbara Basler, "Undercover Resident," *AARP Bulletin*, September 2004.

21. Kathryn Wellin, "Nursing Homes' Silent Pain: Rules Let N.C. Facilities Stay Quiet, Avoid Investigation If Injuries, Deaths Explainable," *Charlotte Observer*, March 14, 2005.

22. "Nurse Pleads Guilty to Reduced Charges of Striking Elderly Patients," *Tribune Review*, March 30, 2005.

23. Erin L. Nissley, "Care Home Death Highlights Holes in System," *Times-Tribune*, August 5, 2007.

24. Janine Reyes, "Allegations of Neglect and Abuse at Nursing Home Questioned," KGBT4, November 19, 2007, http://elderly-abuse.com.

25. Justin Hill, "Provo Nursing Home Cited in Connection with Patient Death," *Daily Herald*, March 1, 2003.

26. "Death of Woman at Nursing Home Probed," *Richmond Times-Dispatch*, August 27, 2004.

27. "State Closes Nursing Home, Says Residents in Danger," *Seattle Times*, April 12, 2003.

28. Erik Schelzig, "Nursing Home Residents Neglected, Review Finds," Associated Press/*Charleston Gazette*, October 9, 2004.

29. Jimmie E. Gates, "Nursing Home Must Pay $10M Award," *Clarion-Ledger*, March 12, 2004.

30. Kevin O'Hanlon, "Nursing Home Sued for Allegedly Poor Care," Associated Press/*Journal Star*, November 23, 2004.

31. Dave Altimari and Kim Martineau, "State Acting in Patient's Death," *Hartford Courant*, January 21, 2005.

32. Gordon Mike, "State to Get $1.7M to Settle Hale Nani Suit," *Honolulu Advertiser*, December 11, 2003.

33. Kauffman Clark, "Former Nursing Home Executive Accused of Plot to Hide Injuries," *Des Moines Register*, March 4, 2005.

34. Amanda J. Crawford, "State Reports More Trouble at Vets Home," *Arizona Republic*, December 8, 2007.

35. Felice J. Freyer, "State Tells Nursing Home to Add Staff," *Providence Journal*, July 20, 2007.

36. Matt Burgard, "Prosecutors Extend Fire Probe Then-Owners of Home Where 16 Died Are under Scrutiny," *Hartford Courant*, April 15, 2005.

37. Alice Dembner, "Grand Jury Probes Death of Nursing Home Resident," *Boston Globe*, March 28, 2005.

38. Holly Edwards, "Inspector Says State Ignored Violations in Nursing Home Fire," *Tennessean*, April 17, 2005.

39. "Wyoming Has High Percentage of Nursing Home Fire Safety Problems," Associated Press/*Casper Star Tribune*, July 26, 2004.

40. Melanie Brandert, "Family Seeks New Prosecutors for Nursing Home Aide," *Baltimore Sun*, October 7, 2003.

41. "Death Tied to Actions of Nursing Home Staff," *Argus Leader*, June 25, 2003.

42. Derrick Nunnally, "Nurse Who Force-Fed 79-Year-Old Patient, Who Died, Gets 13 Months," *Journal Sentinel*, March 18, 2004.

43. Wendy Wendland-Bowyer, "Nursing Home Fight Revived 3 Heat-Wave Deaths Spur New Demand for Air-Conditioning," *Detroit Free Press*, July 6, 2001.

44. Phillip O'Connor, "Two More Families Sue Nursing Home Where Heat Killed Four Federal Officials Also Investigating Deaths at U. City Facility," *St. Louis Today*, June 21, 2001.

45. "Nursing Home Driver Surrenders to Police," Associated Press/*Houston Chronicle*, August 21, 2004.

46. Terri Sanginiti, "Nursing Home Violations Go Unpunished, Panel Told," *News Journal*, May 30, 2003.

47. "Healthcare Temps Should Be Screened," *Daily Advertiser*, December 12, 2007.

48. Mike Casey, "What's Behind the Problems?" *Kansas City Star*, October 17, 2004.

49. Marty Roney, "Nursing Home Patient Raped," *Montgomery Advertiser*, November 6, 2003.

50. "Nursing Home Knew of Visiting Abuser," WMAQ, October 3, 2007, http://elderly-abuse.com.

51. Tom Haydon, "Caretaker of Elderly Accused of Abuse," *Star-Ledger*, November 17, 2004.

52. Tim Bonfield, "Sex Offenders in Nursing Homes," *Cincinnati Enquirer*, July 11, 2004.

53. Finn J. John, "Former Nursing Home Aide Convicted," *Albany Democrat Herald*, June 9, 2004.

54. "Former Nurse Pleads Not Guilty to Abuse," *Burlington Free Press*, June 24, 2004.

55. Eric Weslander, "Nursing Home Worker Checks Can Be Lacking," *Lawrence Journal*, May 31, 2006.

56. Bill Braun, "Care Case Sentence Deferred," *Tulsa World*, March 29, 2005.

57. Chip Guy, "Nursing Home Patient's Family Wins $13M," *News Journal*, March 17, 2005.

58. "Nursing Home Resident Found Dead Outside Facility," *Union Leader*, March 28, 2005.

59. Sabrina Tavernise, "Police Investigate Death of Nursing Home Patient," *New York Times*, February 5, 2004.